"Because of the Hate"
The Murder of Jerry Bailey
By: Kirk McCracken

BECAUSE OF THE HATE

CHAPTER ONE
Thursday, Jan. 22, 1976

Steve Shibley was always late for school. The high school wrestling coach was driving as fast as he could, exceeding the speed limit to get to his first class. It was already 8:30 a.m., and the bell had just sounded. Despite the fact he was a no-nonsense coach, he found it hard to be on time. It had become a running joke that Shibley was always late for school, but the high school administrators weren't laughing. It was mid-January in Oklahoma and the heater in the car finally started to warm up only one block away from the high school. The cold, winter air filled the car again as he rolled down the window to throw out his morning cigarette.

Shibley exhaled, and cigarette smoke came billowing out of his lungs, disappearing out of the car. He rolled up the window as fast as he could, but the inside of the car was cold again and his hands and face were now as cold as they were when he first started the engine in his driveway. "One of These Nights" by the Eagles was on the radio, and the song was just getting to the chorus as Shibley drove closer to the school. He turned up the volume knob and tapped the steering wheel to the beat as the song blared from the car speakers.

That morning was a cool, winter morning filled with the hustle and bustle of parents getting ready for work and kids scurrying off to school. Sapulpa's High School and Elementary schools were surrounded by housing additions, and kids would walk to and from school in groups. Everyone knew when school was about to begin or when it had ended for the day.

Neighborhood dogs would bark as the students walked by the fenced yards. Some dogs barked because they wanted to play and others got a little help from the students that barked back or hit the fence with sticks or rocks, whipping the dogs into a frenzy. The loud sound of school buses would rev up and down the streets as kids yelled at their friends from the tiny rectangular windows of the bright yellow buses.

Sapulpa High School was located in the middle of town and surrounded by middle-class houses. It seemed like every intersection had a stop sign, and Shibley would roll through the sign and then punch the gas only to have to brake immediately for another stop sign. The car's engine would roar and the brakes would screech and neighbors must have thought another student was late for school, driving dangerously through the streets. Shibley was now a block away from the high school. He lived only a few blocks away from the school on N. Moccasin Street, making it even easier to oversleep.

It was then he passed a gray-colored Chevrolet Caprice and recognized the two men inside, fellow coaches Jerry Bailey and Paul Reagor Jr.

Reagor was an assistant football coach and vice principal at Sapulpa High School and Bailey had just resigned as the Sapulpa Chieftain's head football coach after a five-year stint. Reagor's car passed Shibley at the intersection by Holmes Memorial Park, where the football team's playing field and locker rooms were located. It was a block away from the school's campus. The Chieftain football team had just played their final season at that location, and a new stadium and locker room was now located on school grounds. Although Bailey was instrumental in the new facilities, he would never coach at the new stadium because he had just resigned as head coach.

Football season had just ended a few months before and the loose ends were probably still loose. Shibley thought it was a little odd that the two other coaches were driving away from the school right as the first bell rang; after all, Shibley was trying his best to get to school. But there was probably a good reason for it. Bailey could have left his

4

clipboard in his office at the old football field, or maybe they needed to pick up some paperwork or equipment. Not much was stored at Holmes Park anymore.

Shibley's car rolled through the stop sign at the intersection of Watchorn Street and McLoud Street. The wrestling coach waved at the two, and Bailey waved back, but Reagor just nodded his head. Reagor was a large muscular black man, in his early-30s, easily filling the driver's seat without much room to spare. He was easily 250 pounds. Bailey, a white man in his mid-30s, was also in great shape but was a lean 180-plus pounds. The two men were unmistakable.

Shibley could see both men clearly. Bailey was smoking a cigarette and had his cup of coffee in hand. He always had his coffee. After Bailey waved, he smiled and looked straight ahead. Shibley kept driving towards the school, while Reagor's Caprice drove north, heading out of town. The wrestling coach sped through the parking lot, his tires screeching as he stopped in the same space he parked in every morning. His car wasn't even at a complete stop before he jumped out of the driver's side and started walking briskly towards the door of the school. The parking spot was "his," and the students knew not to park there. He quickly walked through the rows of cars to the building, trying to get to his classroom before the morning bell rang.

He wasn't alone. He could see tardy students running towards the building in the same attempt to be on time for class.

"You kids better to get to class before the bell rings," Shibley yelled with a smile on his face. He knew that he wouldn't get detention for being late, but it would be nice to sneak into school without getting caught by any of the principals. He could also say he was trolling the parking lot for students that were late for class. He could, but they wouldn't believe him.

Shibley wasn't a tall man, standing about 5-feet-8-inches, he could have easily blended in with members of the student body if not for the thick, brown mustache that extended to his chin. He didn't look like a typical coach, clean-shaven with a crew cut and pants that were hemmed too high, exposing calf-high white athletic socks. Shibley wore long sideburns with near-shoulder length hair that came close to breaking the school's dress code. He wore bell-bottom pants and shirts that were the latest fashion.

Shibley made it to his classroom with very little time to spare. He sat down at his desk to catch his breath before starting his social studies class. His mind was supposed to be on class. He should have been discussing the differences between hunter-gathers and farmers, or the contributions of ancient civilizations to the modern world. He could be explaining factors that contributed to the decline of the Roman Empire or how technology has the changed the lives of Americans since the Industrial Revolution.

But he couldn't stop thinking about where Bailey and Reagor were headed. It just didn't make sense, but he had students to teach, and he had a wrestling tournament to prepare for later in the day. Shibley's classroom had an outside wall, and he could see the parking lot from rows of windows that nearly went from the ceiling to the floor. As he taught his class during first hour, Shibley kept looking out in the parking lot, waiting for Reagor's car to pull in and park.

In a nearby classroom, Beverly Bailey had already handed out an assignment to her mathematics class. She was in her early-30s, beautiful and blonde, and she'd come with her husband to Sapulpa five years earlier from Nowata, Oklahoma, a smaller community a little more than an hour away. Her husband Jerry Bailey decided to be a football coach long ago, and she had resigned herself to the fact that she would be a coach's wife.

Jerry and Beverly Bailey were both teachers in the Sapulpa school system, while their teen-aged son Guy was in the junior high and their younger daughter Diedra attended Woodlawn Elementary, located on the same square block as the high school and junior high complex. During the day, the Bailey clan was never more than 100 yards away from each other.

When he wasn't on the football field, Jerry taught anatomy and physiology – not your normal football coach/physical education teacher. His classroom was near his wife's in the science wing in the same hallway. Beverly and Dierdre always rode to school together, and Jerry and Guy rode in his El Camino pick-up truck. The Bailey women left the house first, and the Bailey men remained to get ready for the school day.

Beverly had arrived at the high school at about 7:30 a.m., an hour before Shibley saw the two coaches, and she went to the office to check in. The front door was locked, and she had to go through the attendance office to get her attendance papers and any bulletins for the day from the box with her name on it. The mail boxes were just open rectangles that had black plastic labels with each teacher's name embossed in white, making it easier to find in a hurry. Beverly went straight to her mailbox and saw her husband's too. It was right above hers and it was full.

It was always full.

Jerry didn't always check his mailbox, and sometimes his wife had to take the teacher's bulletins to his classroom. During football season he almost never checked, and Beverly always grabbed the papers and placed them on his desk in his classroom. While at home, she always reminded him of the important papers but she knew she would have to grab them the next morning.

She smiled as she looked at the papers that were stuffed in the small box, and she gathered them to take the papers to his classroom, again. This time, the bulletins, papers and letters were crammed in so tight Beverly had to work them out of the small box, removing a few at time to get them out. She licked her lips and grunted as she tugged on the conjoined paperwork. She finally got them out piece by piece and piled them up in a neat stack so she could get them to Jerry's classroom without dropping any.

While Beverly was in the office, she saw attendance clerk Hazel Smith, and they exchanged pleasantries like they did every morning.

"Good morning, Hazel."

"Good morning Mrs. Beverly," Hazel said, looking up from her typewriter.

"It's gonna be cold today. Stay bundled up."

"I sure will. Have a good day, Mrs. Beverly."

Reagor was also in the office milling around aimlessly. Affectionately called "Buck" by the other coaches and teachers, Reagor was lured away from Okmulgee High School by Jerry Bailey to be his offensive line coach at Sapulpa. The town of Okmulgee was located just down Highway 75 south of Sapulpa, and the two schools often played each other in nearly every sport.

Hazel Smith asked Reagor why he was at school so early that morning, but Reagor didn't respond. She also wondered why he missed school the day before; as a matter of fact, Reagor had missed a lot since classes resumed from Christmas break.

He also didn't say anything to Beverly Bailey, which was odd. He must not have seen her because he usually said "Hi" or "Hello" when he saw her. After all, their families were close. They had spent time at each other's houses and had family functions together. Jerry Bailey made sure that his coaching staff was close. They had to be. They spent more time together than with their own families.

Reagor must not have seen her or he had a lot on his mind. Again, he had missed a lot of school since the beginning of the year when classes resumed after the holiday break.

Little more than a month before, Jerry had resigned as the head football coach of the Sapulpa Chieftains. He'd recommended several of his assistant coaches for the position, but someone else was offered the job – someone from outside of the program and from another state. And while Jerry was no longer on staff as a football coach he was going to remain on as a teacher until the end of the year. He assisted in nearly every other sport Sapulpa offered and was still a staple at tennis and wrestling matches, basketball games and track meets.

He did have two boys tennis state championships under his belt at Sapulpa.

After a disappointing run with the Sapulpa Chieftains, Jerry Bailey was ready to move on. He felt he had taken the football program as far as he could and was looking at other coaching jobs around the state, trying to find the perfect fit. He had seen success in other programs, but his time was up at Sapulpa, and he was getting offers from surrounding schools. He thought someone else might be able to take the program farther.

Sapulpa needed a fresh start, and so did Bailey.

Since his resignation, Coach Bailey didn't have to get up at the crack of dawn, trying to figure out ways to score on the Sand Springs Sandite defense, or how to stop high-powered offenses like that of Tulsa Hale, Tulsa Kelley or Tulsa Memorial. He was enjoying a much deserved break after a tough 4-6 season.

During football season, Jerry and his son Guy would leave the house in the morning when it was dark, and return home at night when it was dark. There were always coaches meetings to attend, game films to break-down or wrestling, basketball or baseball games to watch, but now, there was calm in the mornings. For the first time in a long time, Bailey could take time to enjoy his family. He was able to sleep in every morning and get out of bed right before he needed to go to school. It was well deserved. Bailey was coming off a losing season filled with close calls and heart-breaking losses. If a few of the games had gone the other way, Bailey might have hung on and stuck it out, but they hadn't, and he didn't.

Guy Bailey, an athletic 13-year old seventh grader, often got out of bed before his father, Jerry, and got ready for school. He regularly took his father a cup of coffee to drink while getting ready for the day, and this day wasn't any different.

Coach Bailey put on his red, blue and white, plaid bell-bottom pants, blue button-up, long-sleeved dress shirt and his blue leather jacket. The two got into Bailey's El Camino pick-up at around 8:10 a.m., backed out of the driveway past the well-manicured lawn, and through their upscale neighborhood toward the high school. The Bailey's lived about a mile south of the high school and the drive didn't take very long. It was only about five minutes if the two stop lights between the school and the house were red.

The school was only a few minutes away, giving the father and son a chance to talk about sports, and Guy received pointers on things that he needed to work on before his junior high basketball game later that day. Guy was quite the basketball player, and his father helped coach whatever team he was on. Jerry Bailey could be seen helping with the wrestling, tennis, basketball and track teams in both the junior high and high school.

The two arrived at Sapulpa High School and parked in the back of the school by the new football locker room and the new stadium – George F. Collins Stadium. Both structures were still under construction, and both were due to the tireless efforts of Bailey and his coaching staff.

Before the new George F. Collins Stadium, the Chieftains played football at Holmes Park, located at Hobson and Adams Streets, just a block away. There was a full city block of houses that separated the school and the football field. The old football complex was named after former Sapulpa schools superintendent Joe R. Holmes, and the new stadium would don the name of its generous benefactor, George Fulton Collins. The Collins family gave about $100,000 in 1975 for the new stadium and the rest of the money was approved through a school bond that was voted on by the community. It is still named George F. Collins Stadium to this day, and it received its first real facelift in 2016, about 40 years after it held its first official game.

Bailey parked in the exact same spot that he did every morning near the new locker room. He put his car keys under the floor mat on the driver's side, grabbed his clipboard, and the father and son headed toward the school.

The clipboard had Bailey's papers and personal information that involved his search for a new coaching job. He called it his "job-getting kit." Despite his rocky time at Sapulpa, the head coach was in demand and considered one of the best in the state, and he was being courted by several other schools. He did have a football state championship under his belt at a different high school. He had jumped from Class 2A to 4A when he accepted the job at Sapulpa, and the game was different. The football players were bigger, faster, and the opposing schools had more players to choose from. The bigger schools had bigger football budgets, but that meant bigger expectations and more politics.

As the two Baileys were walking toward the school, they came across Paul Reagor.

"Hey, Guy, how are ya?" Reagor said to the teen.

"Just fine," the younger Bailey answered. Guy was walking fast because he didn't want to be late for school, but he did hear a little bit of the conversation between Reagor and his father.

"Hey, Jerry, what are you planning on doin' now? Have any coaching jobs lined up?" Reagor asked.

"I've got a few, Buck," Bailey said. "I'm just weighing my options to see what feels right."

By now Guy was out of earshot, but his father and the former assistant coach kept talking. The two coaches walked towards the school and entered the doors by the high school cafeteria. Almost immediately, Reagor asked Bailey if he would go for a drive with him so they could talk. Bailey agreed, and the two men started walking back to the parking lot.

Sophomore football player Terry Holbrook saw the two coaches as he walked out of the door near the cafeteria. Holbrook was hurrying to class and he said "Hello" to his coaches. Bailey smiled and Reagor said "Hello." The two coaches just kept walking and didn't stop to talk to Holbrook, a tall, white, athletic underclassman. Holbrook didn't like Reagor much. The assistant coach didn't really mess with him during practice, but some of the other football players weren't as lucky, and Holbrook just didn't like him.

The coaches got into Reagor's Caprice and drove out of the parking lot.

Moments later, the two men drove by Coach Shibley. Bailey noticed the wrestling coach and waved. Bailey also smiled and shook his head. He knew Shibley was late for school and it was funny to him. Shibley was always late for school.

*****

First period was unremarkable for most of the classes except one. The bell rang, ending first period, and a second class of students filed into Beverly's classroom. One of her students, a football player, trudged past her desk.

"Coach Bailey's substitute teacher never showed up," he said to Beverly, realizing he might have just ruined it for the rest of Coach Bailey's classes.

"What substitute?" she asked puzzled.

"The one for first hour. Is Coach Bailey sick or something?"

Beverly was confused. "You mean he wasn't there?"

"No. We were in class all hour without a sub," he said with a smile on his face. It was obvious Bailey's first hour class had been a free-for-all since there wasn't a teacher or a substitute watching over them.

Beverly started her students on the same assignment as her first hour class and told them she was going down the hall to her husband's classroom. She warned them she would not put up with any bad behavior and that they needed to work quietly. That meant no talking and no getting up from their desks. As she opened the door and looked in, Beverly found a room full of noisy students, unsupervised, and her husband was nowhere to be found. She told the rowdy classroom to keep the noise down. She didn't tell the class where she was going, but she headed to the office to use the telephone to call home.

On the way down the hall, she wondered if he'd been sick and had gone back home. He seemed fine earlier that morning and nothing had been wrong the night before. She reached the office, picked up the phone and dialed home. She didn't greet Secretary Hazel Smith like she had earlier that morning. She quickly dialed her home number on the tan rotary phone, waiting for the dial to go back to zero. She let the phone ring longer than she normally would, hoping Jerry would pick up, but no one answered.

Steve Shibley had made it through first hour and had started his second class of the day when assistant football coach Jerry Dean opened the door to Shibley's classroom and motioned for him to come into the hallway, out of earshot of the students. Dean wanted to talk to him in private without the students hearing their conversation. He didn't want to start any unnecessary rumors about Jerry, but he wanted to see if Shibley knew why Jerry wasn't in his classroom.

"Hey Shib, have you seen Jerry or Buck?" Dean whispered. "No one's seen them."

Dean wasn't just one of Bailey's assistant football coaches. He was his friend – his best friend. The two had been born and raised in Broken Bow, Oklahoma where they lived less than a mile apart and were virtually inseparable growing up. They played football together and when they graduated from high school, both went to Southeastern Oklahoma State University in Durant, Oklahoma on football scholarships. After college, they started coaching together, and why not? They had been together since childhood, but now, Dean had no idea where his best friend was.

"I saw them this morning," Shibley said.

"You're kidding? Where?" Dean said in disbelief.

"When I passed the football field on my way here. Looked like they were headed out of town," Shibley said.

"Out of town? Well, they never showed, and Bev is covering Jerry's class, but she can't do that all day," Dean said.

Shibley sighed, "Let me know if you hear anything. I'll be in the gym this afternoon, getting ready for this weekend's tournament."

Dean nodded and headed back down the hall. Shibley walked back into his classroom, but his mind wasn't on teaching history. He had a wrestling tournament to prepare for and his friend wasn't where he was supposed to be. All of the students looked at their teacher as he walked back to his desk, but they didn't hear his conversation with Dean. However, they could tell by the look on his face that something wasn't right.

* * * * *

When she didn't get an answer at home, Beverly went back to her husband's classroom, hoping to find him there.

But there was nothing but unruly students, and Coach Bailey hadn't ever showed. She put aside her anxiety and got to work, covering both classes herself, going between the two rooms and praying that wherever he was, Jerry was all right. And if he was, he had better have one hell of an excuse.

At 11 a.m., more than an hour after she found out her husband wasn't at school, Sapulpa High School Vice Principal Ron James opened the door to Beverly's classroom and asked her to step outside. He normally knocked, but this couldn't wait. James stood in the doorway with his hand behind him, keeping the door propped open.

"Beverly, I need to talk to you outside," James said.

If Dean and Shibley's conversation was one the students didn't need to hear, this conversation needed to be even more confidential.

His eyes were fixed on Beverly as she told her class to work on their geometry assignment and to not talk while she was gone. They students wouldn't dare, Mr. James was standing right there and he wasn't to be messed with.

It was now third hour, and she followed the vice principal into the hall and James immediately started asking questions.

"Beverly, Jerry's not in his classroom. Do you know where he is?"

"I don't know," she said. "He isn't in the office with you?" she said in a hopeful but confused voice.

"No," James said. He spoke with a soft, concerned voice, trying to soften the blow of the news she was about to receive. "Beverly, there's a policeman in the office, and he said he wants to talk to you."

James wasn't a tall man, but he commanded respect from students and teachers and normally got it. He was stern, but fair and always had time to listen to the student's concerns. James was in charge of discipline and could hold his own if he needed to break up a fight or get his bluff in on an unruly student. He was going bald on top of his head but had a large amount of golden blond hair on the sides.

Beverly didn't seem concerned, just a little confused. She followed James down the hall. It was a long walk. As he passed the blue lockers, he looked up at the basketball team's hand-painted paper banners taped to the walls that read:

"Chieftains are #1"

"SHS Rocks!"

"Chieftains chop the Trojans"

It was now basketball and wrestling season and last football season was just a distant memory.

As he read the banners, James was thinking of where the coaches could be, praying they were safe, and if they were, they had better have one hell of an excuse. He was looking down at the blue and white checkered tiles on the floor, and the clacking of his dress shoes echoed through the hallway. Beverly's heels were also making a lighter clacking sound, and despite having shorter legs than Mr. James, she was keeping up with him stride for stride. As they got closer to the office, the clacking noise grew louder and louder. Nothing was said between the two, and James couldn't take the sound of their shoes any longer. The sound was pounding in his head like a drummer with perfect rhythm. That drummer was also playing a drum solo in his chest. His heart was beating so fast and so loud it felt like it would beat out of his body, and he had to say something.

He knew he shouldn't say anything yet but he couldn't wait to get to the office. The words came rushing out and James told Beverly everything he knew so far. He had to prepare her for what the police officer was going to tell her.

"Beverly, the police found some of Jerry's papers on the side of the road, and they think something is wrong," James said.

"I don't understand," she said.

"Beverly, the papers had blood on them."

The police had found some of Jerry's papers, the same papers he'd carried that morning on his clipboard, and Jerry was officially listed as missing by the police. Actually, both coaches were listed as missing. Earlier that morning, Shibley had seen Jerry Bailey with Paul Reagor, but neither could be found. The papers from her husband's "job-getting kit" were the only clue to his possible whereabouts. Just before 11 a.m., Jerry's papers had been found on the side of the road near South Mingo Road and 121st Street in Bixby in southern Tulsa County. Bixby was a neighboring town of Sapulpa and it is located about 20 miles away. Sapulpa is in Creek County, and it would take around 35 minutes to drive to Bixby. To get to Bixby, the coaches would have more than likely driven through Kiefer or through Glenpool. The towns of Sapulpa and Bixby didn't share a city limits sign, but they weren't that far away from each other.

Bixby police handed the evidence over to Sapulpa law enforcement. The departments started to work together to conduct a search for the missing men and the car they were last seen in.

"How do they know they were HIS papers?" Beverly said.

"They had his name on them. That's all we know right now. Talk to these officers and answer their questions. Beverly, it's going to be OK," James said, but he wasn't sure it was going to be OK.

Beverly walked into the office and, by then, several police officers and detectives had gathered. They closed the door and started asking her questions, but she did not have the answers.

No one outside of the office could make out what they were taking about. The muffled conversation was inaudible due to the cinder block walls and thick wooden doors, but you could hear a pin drop outside of the office. The secretarial staff and students in the office all knew something was very wrong, but they didn't know what it could be.

To Vice Principal James, Beverly didn't seem distressed, either out of confusion or denial. During football seasons, the coaches were always out of pocket. They would take game film to a developer in Tulsa and hang out at a local watering hole until the film was developed. It took several hours, and then the coaches went back to the school to break down the film in the coach's office. Of course, that only happened after football games on Friday nights and not during school hours. Football season was long over, and there was no reason for him to be gone from school. He wasn't in his classroom, and she knew he would never leave his students without a good reason.

The information didn't add up, and no one seemed to be able to process it all. The town of Bixby is less than 20 miles away, and the papers were with Jerry that morning. How did the papers get all the way to Bixby, and why were the coaches there instead of the high school?

Football coaches would often exchange game films with other teams, but again, football season was over.

Knowing something was definitely wrong, the high school principals sent for Jerry and Beverly's children, Guy and Diedra, so the family could be together. The three Baileys were taken to their house on Courtney Street about four or five blocks from the school. In the back of her mind, Beverly wondered if someone had called Reagor's' wife, Emma Jean, and how she was taking the news that her husband was also missing.

Sapulpa Police contacted Emma Jean, a homeroom teacher at John Paul Jones Elementary School in Tulsa, but she had no idea what could have happened to her husband, and she couldn't think of any appointments that would take him away from school. She said her husband left the house early that morning like normal, and nothing was out of the ordinary. However, Emma Jean wasn't always forthcoming with the school about her husband and his absences from school. He had been gone the day before, and he had missed several days at the beginning of January for a very specific reason, but, as of this morning, Emma Jean said her husband had treated it like any other.

The same was said about Bailey. It was business as usual as the Baileys got ready for school that day.

Meanwhile, reporters at the Sapulpa Daily Herald newspaper found out about the missing coaches and published a story for the Thursday edition. The headline read:

"2 Missing."

Bloody transcripts and other personal papers belonging to Jerry Bailey were found Thursday near Bixby and officials said the recently-resigned Sapulpa High School football coach and SHS Vice Principal Paul Reagor were feared missing.

Witnesses reported seeing Bailey get into a car with a man believed to be Reagor at about 8:15 a.m. Thursday at the school parking lot. Neither was at school after classes began.

Bixby officers notified Sapulpa Police at mid-morning that a clipboard and manila envelope with fresh blood on it were found on Mingo Road between 121st and 131st Street.

Bixby officers said a search of the area was being conducted.

District Attorney David Young, Superintendent of schools, Dr. John Martin and Principal Charles Dodson met with Sapulpa Police at mid-morning.

Bailey's wife Beverly, also a teacher at the high school, said she and their daughter left early for school Thursday and Bailey left home later with their son Guy, a junior high student. Bailey's car was in the parking lot.

Bailey resigned as Sapulpa head coach after the past season but remained as a teacher. Reagor was an assistant coach the past season.

By the time the paper hit newsstands, the coaches had been missing for only a few hours, but the bloody papers were a concern to law enforcement. The newspaper report only fueled speculation, and rumors were spreading all over town about what could have happened to the two missing coaches. Had they been kidnapped? Had they been in a car accident? Had they been in the wrong place at the wrong time? Did they go help someone in need, only to have met with a horrible fate? No one knew for sure, but one thing was for certain: the two coaches seemed to have vanished into thin air.

Steve Shibley was supposed to begin preparing for Sapulpa's annual wrestling tournament, but early in the day, the head wrestling coach had put the preparations aside, making phone calls to see if anyone had seen Bailey or Reagor. Shibley called everyone he knew, more than 50 calls in all, before finally returning his attention to the tournament, a tournament that Jerry Bailey helped maintain. A few years earlier, Shibley wanted to discontinue the tournament because larger schools were opting out of it and the event became more of a "B" team or junior varsity tournament. However, Bailey convinced Shibley to keep it going. Bailey got on the phone and started working his magic. He invited the larger schools again, and they couldn't say "no" -- not to Jerry Bailey.

Later Thursday night, Sapulpa High School Principal Charles Dodson informed Shibley that the wrestling tournament would be canceled due to the missing coaches. Shibley was furious and felt that Bailey would have wanted the tournament to go on. After all, no one knew where the coaches were, and no one knew what had happened to them. For Shibley, his wrestlers had been working day in and day out for this tournament, making weight, training and lifting weights, and it wouldn't be canceled without a damn good reason. Dodson wouldn't budge, but neither would Shibley, so he moved the wrestling mats to the high school gym to prepare for the event. Shibley was known for not bowing under the pressure of anyone, even if they were his superiors. He always did what he thought was best, which helped eventually earn him the school's athletic director position in the 1980s.

Police officials from Bixby, Sapulpa and Tulsa conducted a massive search, but by dark that night, the search hadn't revealed anything, and it was called off until the morning. Several people weren't about to turn in for the night. Assistant coach Jerry Dean and Oklahoma Highway Patrolman Kent Thomsen decided to keep looking even though it was dark. They searched all over the towns of Sapulpa, Jenks, Glenpool and parts of Bixby. They had no idea at the time, but later, they would discover they were very close to Reagor and Bailey during the night search. However, there was simply no chance of finding them in the dark.

The two men weren't just looking for a fellow Sapulpan; they were looking for a friend. Bailey, Thomsen, Dean, teachers Bill Shaw, Antwine Pryor, Steve Shibley and former high school principal John Cockrum played cards every Wednesday night at Shaw's house. With the exception of Trooper Thomsen, they were all teachers or coaches and no one ever missed the card game. But this wasn't about the game. It was about the camaraderie and the friendship between the poker players. It didn't matter if money changed hands. They were there as friends, but money did exchange hands.

Friday, Jan. 23, 1976

Early the next morning, right after daybreak, the massive search resumed with officers from across the area.

The same people that were searching late into the night were back searching again with even more fervor than before. If the two coaches were hurt, they probably needed medical attention, immediately. If they were in a ditch somewhere, they needed help. They had to be found.

The Tulsa World newspaper, Oklahoma's biggest newspaper on the eastern side of the state, picked up on the missing person's report after deadline on Thursday and printed a story about the coaches the following day. The Sapulpa Daily Herald was an afternoon paper, but the Tulsa World, also a daily newspaper, was a morning paper and they went to press in the middle of the night. The story about the missing coaches appeared in the Friday, Jan. 23, 1976 edition with the headline:

Sapulpa Teacher's Missing; Blood Found on Papers
By Tom Wood
SAPULPA – A batch of blood stained papers found near Bixby has caused Police to fear that ex-Sapulpa football coach Jerry Bailey and his former assistant, Paul Reagor Jr. both missing have run into foul play.

The two men were last seen at 8:15 a.m. Thursday on Sapulpa High School's parking lot, according to Chief of Police Johnny Moore. Moore said Bailey got out of his pick-up truck and got into Reagor's car. They drove off together.

Dispatcher Claudia Alcorn said Bixby Police called Sapulpa about 10:26 a.m. and reported finding Bailey's papers east of Bixby.

"They didn't suspect foul play until the papers with blood on them were found," the dispatcher said. "Now we have about 20 men out searching the area. Tulsa Police have entered the case and joined forces with Bixby," the dispatcher said.

She described the papers as personal, including one paper which Bailey evidently had written personally.

Moore said Bixby police found the papers on Mingo Road strewn between 111ᵗʰ and 131ˢᵗ Streets.

Bailey, 33, (he was 34) *who teaches science, had earned a reputation of building winning teams when he was coach of the Nowata Ironmen before coming here in 1971. His teams were successful in Sapulpa his first few years* (They weren't. Bailey won three games each in his first two seasons at Sapulpa). *Last year, however, he had a 2-8 season* (Sapulpa was 2-8 in 1974 and 4-6 in 1975). *He resigned as a coach but stayed on as a teacher.*

A Broken Bow High School graduate, Bailey was an all-Oklahoma Collegiate Conference split receiver at Southeastern State College in Durant.

Reagor, 32, who lives at 4307 E. 51ˢᵗ St. Tulsa, also resigned his coaching position and became vice principal of the school.

"We are just in shock," Supt. John Martin said.

"We don't have any idea of what could have happened."

Martin said as far as he knew "there was no ill-will whatsoever," between Bailey and Reagor.

The Bixby area search was called off because of darkness, police said. It is to be resumed Friday morning.

The Tulsa County Sheriff's Department requested an aerial search of south Tulsa County and Creek County. Medivac helicopter pilot Steve McKim began the aerial search of the area.

Local newsmen Ed Poston and Red Stattum, of KTUL Channel 8 in Tulsa, were informed by a Jenks police officer that law enforcement officials were searching Bixby and Jenks and the two newsmen joined the search as well, driving around the two towns.

They were given the description of the missing car, the tag number, and where the two coaches were last seen together. Ed Poston worked in several capacities for the news channel, including reporter, assignment editor and weekend sports anchorman. Red Stattum was Poston's cameraman, and Poston had previous experience in law enforcement. Before joining the Army, he was a reserve sheriff's deputy in Kansas while attending college. He then joined the Army and worked for the Armed Forces Radio and Television Division as a correspondent in Berlin. The two newsmen noticed the Medivac helicopter and flagged it down in order to get on board to film the area for the news. Both newsmen knew McKim and he obliged, allowing the two on board. It was a tight fit in the helicopter, but they had to make it work.

Poston told himself he wouldn't ever get back in a helicopter after his discharge from the Army, but he needed to get in the air to assist in the search and get some aerial shots for the news. He hated helicopters.

Stattum was shooting 16-mm film. Video tape wasn't used at that time, so it was common for news crews to have two separate rolls running at once; one roll for film, and the other for sound. They had to haul around a lot of equipment, and it had to be stuffed into an already cramped helicopter.

The helicopter was searching south Tulsa County in the Jenks and Bixby areas just before noon when the crew saw a car matching the description of Reagor's car in some tall weeds near an abandoned farm house at 145th Street and Mingo Road in Bixby.

"Is that the car?" Poston yelled into the headphones so Stattum could hear him over the rotation of the loud helicopter blades. He pointed at the car and shrugged.

"I think so," Stattum said with excitement in his voice.

"We need to find a clearing to land," McKim said looking in every direction to find a flat patch of land, free from telephone or electrical lines. There were some telephone and power lines near the road, and there were trees around the farmhouse. Poston then noticed an empty field.

"Set her down in that field over there and we'll get a better look," Poston yelled into the headset, pointing to the field adjacent to the farmhouse.

From the air, the tire tracks leading to the car looked fresh, as if someone had recently driven through the weeds to get to the house, a small two-bedroom abandoned farmhouse that had obviously been empty for some time. The weeds had grown high, making it hard to see exactly what was around the house. The car had not been visible from the road, making it impossible for searchers on the ground to have seen it. Trooper Thomsen and Coach Dean had probably driven by the farmhouse several times while searching the night before.

The Medivac pilot landed the helicopter safely, and Poston and Stattum hopped out and approached the car. Poston identified the charcoal gray Chevrolet Caprice by its license tag: OM-9171. They had found Reagor's car. There was a handprint visible in the dust on the lid of the trunk. It appeared to be a fresh handprint, but there was something else on the bumper of the car that concerned the two newsmen.

They noticed smeared, dried blood on the bumper of the car just under the handprint. The blood was dried but it was clear to the reporters the blood hadn't been there long. It was still red but starting to turn to a brown rust color. The blood wasn't fresh but it wasn't old either. Poston had a feeling that someone was inside the trunk of the car. He ran to the Imperial Apartments across the street, his heart racing with every footstep. He told the security guard of the apartments to call the police. He didn't even say why, but the security guard knew he had better do as he was told. Poston then called his office at Channel 8 to inform them that they had found the car of the missing coaches.

Poston went back to the house and, being a former police officer, realized they were standing in the middle of a potential crime scene. He encouraged everyone to move back from the area and wait for the police to arrive. He didn't want to destroy any evidence.

The call to the Tulsa County Sheriff's Department prompted a large number of officers from different towns and departments to the location. At noon, Sapulpa Police Officers Richard Johnson, Tom Clark, Joe Collins and Oklahoma Highway Patrolman Thomsen arrived at the scene. Thomsen was in the area still looking for his friend and saw the helicopter flying in the area several times. He then got the call on his police radio that Reagor's car had been found. Thomsen turned on his lights and siren and headed for the house as fast has his car could go.

As Thomsen's black and white patrol car raced down the road, the trooper was confused. No information had been given over the radio, and he had to get to the scene to find out what happened to his friend. Was the car abandoned? Stolen? Wrecked? Broken down on the side of the road? Had it been in an accident?

Thomsen was only 32 years old, but he had the experience of a seasoned veteran. He started with the Oklahoma Highway Patrol in 1969 and had been on the job for about seven years when the murder occurred.

At the farm house, Sapulpa Police Officer Johnson moved in to investigate the car parked in the tall weeds. He tried to open the doors but they were locked, preventing him from entering the vehicle. The police searched the outside and underneath of the vehicle, looking for the keys. He also saw the dried blood on the bumper, but that was all they had as far as evidence. They still did not know where the two coaches were.

The officers asked for a wire coat hanger to try and pry open the trunk or to snag the door's latch through the window. Thomsen arrived at the scene, and his car slid to a stop on the gravel driveway, kicking up a grey mist of dust. He immediately sprang into action. He asked the officers what they knew, and they showed him the dried blood. The trooper needed to get into that trunk.

Thomsen, whose kids would eventually attend Sapulpa schools, stopped and took a breath. How could he get into that car without just pulling the trunk's lid off with his bare hands? Thomsen was a large, muscular man who filled out every inch of his two-tone brown trooper uniform, and he could have pulled off that trunk lid if no other ideas came to mind.

He saw the car keys hanging in the ignition. He needed those keys to get into the back of the car. All of the doors were locked, but the passenger side door hadn't been completely shut. Older cars did not have complex locking systems. It was all manual, and they could be popped easily. Someone with great dexterity and a coat hanger could pull back the window and hook the lock with the hanger, pulling up quickly to unlock the door. But Thomsen didn't have that kind of time.

Breaking the window was the last option because it could destroy evidence. He didn't want to break the window with a Billy club, but he would if he had to.

Thomsen pushed on the door until the lock popped up. He reached through the passenger side door, retrieved the keys from the ignition, and walked to the back of the car. Thomsen wanted to find his friend, but if Jerry Bailey was in the trunk, Thomsen knew he would be dead.

It was eerily quiet. The trooper could hear the crunch of the dead weeds and grass under his boots as he walked to the back of the car. The crunch sounded louder than normal, and the wind was swirling and howling around him, blocking out the whispered conversations as the officers and news crew also started to walk towards the car's trunk.

Thomsen could feel his heart in his chest, and he could hear his lungs inhale and exhale, but it was shaky as if his heart was beating so fast and so hard that it interfered with his breathing.

He slid the key in the trunk's lock and turned it until he heard a pop that lifted the lid about an inch or two. He lifted it a few more inches and hesitated for a second or two before convincing himself to open the trunk. He lifted the lid with his shaking hands and groaned, "Awe, Jerry."

Jerry Bailey's lifeless body was crammed into the dirty trunk. He was dressed in the same clothes he had worn to school the day before, but now he was covered in blood from multiple stab wounds to his abdomen and back.

CHAPTER TWO
JERRY BAILEY

Jerry Bailey was born December 18, 1941 in the rural Oklahoma town of Broken Bow. He was the third of four children born to Obie and Rhea Bailey, but the family moved to Orange, Texas soon after his birth to help with the war effort during World War II. Jerry had an older brother Kenneth and an older sister Martha. A younger sister Sandra was born while the family lived in Texas. After the Japanese attack on Pearl Harbor in 1941, Jerry's father Obie wanted to help his country and worked in a shipyard until the war was over.

Orange, Texas, a town located on the banks of Sabine River near the Gulf of Mexico, was lucky to even be a town after the depression. Despite several lumber and a shipping yards, the town was floundering and in need of something to help revive the once thriving town.

For the next several years, the Bailey family moved around until settling back in the town Jerry was born in. Broken Bow -- a town of about 4,000 people -- is located in southeast Oklahoma and is a gateway city to Broken Bow Lake, Beavers Bend Resort Park, the Mountain Fork, Glover Rivers and the Ouachita National Forest. The town also borders Texas and Arkansas.

Broken Bow was a close knit community and everyone knew each other. There were always picnic lunches and church socials that usually involved a fiddle or guitar, and every October, the town got together to slaughter pigs for the winter. Summers were hot, and ponds were usually filled with kids trying to cool down after a long day of playing in the hills or a baseball double-header.

The Bailey's wood-frame farmhouse sat on 160 acres and had a log cabin barn that housed several animals, including sheep, cattle, pigs, chickens, rabbits and a milking cow.

The Bailey children had chores, and everyone had to do their part. Whether it was feeding the animals, cleaning the barn, picking berries and apples, working in the garden or canning vegetables for the winter, everyone had work to do.

Obie encouraged his children to be competitive and thought it was healthy. He used sawdust and extra lumber from the saw mill to build a running track in the back yard. The farm house also had a basketball goal and three-on-three basketball games could break out at any time.

Jerry was easy-going and quiet, but he had an ornery streak, and his smile was legendary. He did well in school and had a growing interest in mathematics. Before high school, Jerry was told he was too small to play varsity football, and it reminded him of something his father had been telling him since he was a little boy, "You can do anything you want to, if you want it bad enough."

Jerry wanted it bad.

He began eating everything he could get his hands on and started a workout regimen that included weight lifting and running. Jerry made the high school football team and became one of the best players on the squad.

By the time Jerry and his sister Sandra were in high school, in the mid-1950s, his family opened a restaurant in town. When the state track meet was held in Broken Bow, none of the restaurants would serve the black athletes. Schools that had black athletes couldn't eat in the restaurants, but the coaches could buy the food and serve them on the team bus or they could eat outside behind the building.

The Bailey's didn't feel the same way and welcomed everyone no matter what color they were. Pretty soon, all of the teams with black players were eating at the Bailey's restaurant without the threat of violence or racism.

Jerry graduated from Broken Bow High School in 1959 and was a stand-out wide receiver and lineman on the football team, and Broken Bow Savage fans will say that his game against Heavner High School in 1958 was his best. Heavner was undefeated thanks to star football player John Tatum, who later played center at the University of Oklahoma.

Tatum was the work horse for the Heavner Wolves, carrying the bulk of the load at fullback his senior season. He played center and linebacker his sophomore and junior seasons but was picked to be the team's main ball carrier as a senior. Tatum played with tremendous heart due to the fact that he was sick a lot as a child. He had a slight case of polio, contracted malaria once and was plagued with severe allergies when he was younger.

When the highly-touted fullback was handed the ball against Broken Bow, he was hit immediately. Everyone knew Tatum was going to get the ball, but it was one defender in particular that met Tatum at the line of scrimmage nearly every single play. That defender was Jerry Bailey.

As Tatum lay on the ground, Jerry Bailey would be there, extending his hand to help the star fullback off of the ground. Of course, it was Bailey that put him there play after play. He would knock him down and help him back up again.

Bailey then went on to play football at Southeastern State College – located in Durant, Oklahoma – making waves as a Savage once again. His college football team had the exact same mascot as his high school, the Savages. It is very common for Oklahoma high schools to adopt Indian mascots like Chieftains, Savages, Warriors, Redskins, etc.

At Southeastern State, Bailey was recruited as a lineman, but the coaching staff had recruited one of the best passing quarterbacks in the area in Oklahoma City U.S. Grant's Duke Christian. The only problem was the team didn't have any receivers that could catch passes from

Christian. Bailey noticed this and brought it to the attention of the Savage coaching staff.

In football, the expression "put up or shut up" is widely used, and Bailey did just that. His coach told him that if he thought they needed a receiver, he should do it. He did, earning Oklahoma Intercollegiate All-Conference honors as a tight end in 1962. He graduated in 1963 as did Christian, who went onto to be named the head coach at Southeastern in 1971, and Christian was inducted into the college's athletic hall of fame in 1989.

Rumor has it Bailey was going to sign a free agent contract to play in the NFL with the Detroit Lions as a receiver, but he decided to become a teacher, coach, husband and father. He and Beverly were married in college, and they were well on their way to a family by the time he could have played professional football.

He took his first coaching job at Atoka High School as an assistant under head coach Vern Robertson. Atoka was just down the highway from his college town of Durant. Bailey then became a head coach with stints at Ada and Seminole before landing at Fairfax in 1968, guiding the Yellow Jackets to a 7-3 record in his first year. However, his first year would be his only year there, and he finally headed north, accepting the vacant head-coaching job at Nowata, Oklahoma in 1969.

In his first year at Nowata, he started the season off winless in the first seven games, but finished the season with three-straight wins for a 3-6-1 record.

After the disappointing losing season, the 1970 season started out a lot like the year before, but it ended very different.

Bailey was no-nonsense on the field and demanded the best out of his players, but he was also known as a player's coach. He was a coach that also cared about what was going on in his player's lives off of the field.

On Tuesday, Dec. 15, 1970, Sapulpa head football coach John Scott stepped down from the position, but stayed on as a history teacher until the end of the year. Scott, a Wewoka native, came to Sapulpa in 1964 from Morland, Kansas and was hired as an assistant for the Chieftains. He was named head coach of the Chieftains only three years later in 1967.

Scott played for the Wewoka Tigers in high school and played in the 1956 All-State game and the Oil Bowl, where the Texans beat the Sooners 37-0 in the high school all-star contest. In the 1956 All-State game, he played against Sapulpans Dickie Young and Don French, and Oklahoma Sooner great Prentice Gault.

He played college football at Oklahoma A&M College, Northeastern A&M and East Central State. While head coach at Sapulpa, Scott tallied a 14-26-1 record in four years and had his best year in 1970 with a 5-6 record. The Chieftains started off with a 5-1 record with wins over Broken Arrow (9-0), Sand Springs (30-7), Cushing (24-3), Webster (14-12) and Oklahoma City Northeast (18-2).

Through six games, Sapulpa had only lost to Pryor 38-7, but the Chieftains lost their last four games for a 5-6 losing record. The team lost their last three games by a total score of 86-8, including two shutouts (21-0 to Stillwater and 19-0 to Miami) to end the season.

Scott's career at Sapulpa culminated in one of the highest honors a coach could receive in Oklahoma. He was selected as a member of the North coaching staff for the Oklahoma All-State football game the following summer. The coaching honor made a complete cycle for Scott, who participated for the 1956 South team while in high school.

Sapulpa then hired Jerry Bailey as the new head coach on Monday, February 1, 1971 in hopes that the young coach could revive a once powerful football program. Since the undefeated season of 1951, the Chieftains compiled only eight winning seasons to 11 losing seasons and most were only by a game or two. Sapulpa had also earned three-straight losing seasons in Scott's last three years.

Bailey, the then 29-year old head coach talked to the Sapulpa Daily Herald for the Monday, February 1, 1971 edition of the paper about his own expectations at the new position.

"I view this job as an opportunity here, and I have a lot to try to do. It will be my obligation to teach football to the people who want to learn. I don't believe in recruiting. I sell the game of football. Football should teach an athlete to have class, and the ability to go out and get what he wants.

"I don't want to be popular," he said. "But I will be honest. If a boy is willing to put out what it takes, I think we can have a good football team. It's a question of personality and class, more team ideas than everything else. Football is an unusual sport. Each of the 11 people has something to get done, and he must do it for the team to get the job done."

Bailey was also known for being a little superstitious. He had a buckeye that he kept in his pocket, and it had to accompany him to every game.

A buckeye is a nut from the buckeye tree which looks like a buck's eye and has been reported, for the past two centuries, to bring good luck to those who carry it. The nut has a shiny outside shell that gleams and shines the more you rub or touch it.

The poisonous nut can be used for luck in any aspect of life, but is reportedly used mainly by sports fans. He also had a lucky pair of coaching shoes. His black leather dress shoes were also a staple in Bailey's attire, and he would wear them to every game.

At games, Bailey and his coaching staff dressed as if they were going to a Sunday morning church service. The staff always wore dress shirts, coats, slacks and ties, and Bailey could often be seen wearing a sweater-like cardigan or a satin football jacket over his dress shirt and tie.

When Bailey moved to a new town, the first thing he did was to find the town's First Baptist Church. For Bailey, it was church and family first, and everything else was secondary.

Bailey was also known for his hospitality and kindness outside of football. When Ronald James was hired as the Sapulpa High School assistant principal, one of the first people he met was Coach Bailey.

Ronald James and his wife Iris, also a teacher, were walking in their neighborhood when Bailey and his wife stopped to introduce themselves to get more acquainted with the new residents. The Baileys were driving Jerry's El Camino truck, and all four crammed into the front seat of the two-seater vehicle. The new friends drove around town and the James' were shown the sights of Sapulpa and introduced to several of the Bailey's friends.

In most cases, football coaches teach history, which consists of telling their class to read their textbooks while they read the sports page of the local newspaper. Most coaches are judged by their teams' performance on the field and not their performance in the classroom.

Bailey was different.

There weren't many teachers that taught Anatomy and Physiology and knew what they were talking about. It is very rare to find a coach that knows as much about science as he does opposing defenses. He was just as concerned about his students in the classroom as he was about his players on the field.

The closest that Bailey ever got to bringing football into his classroom was in Nowata when he had the female students sew the holes in the game uniforms while he was lecturing about science. At times, it looked like he was teaching home economics.

When he first arrived at Sapulpa, Bailey was appalled at the condition of the athletic facilities, and it was obvious to him why the Chieftains were having trouble competing in the largest class in Oklahoma at the time – Class 4A. The poor facilities brought out the promoter in Bailey, and the new coach was able to acquire funds and materials through donations, and the result was the locker room that now bears his name. Bailey started making changes immediately after getting the head-coaching job at Sapulpa.

CHAPTER THREE
The Crime Scene

In the trunk, Bailey's body was lying on several jugs of anti-freeze, a couple of green and white folded lawn chairs, a spare tire, an air pump, several aerosol cans, a glass bottle, paper sacks and lots of paper. It was the same paper from his clip board or "job-getting kit." He was lying on his left side facing the open trunk with his left arm underneath his head. He used his hand as a make-shift pillow, and it looked like he was sleeping.

It seemed he tried to make himself as comfortable as possible, waiting for someone to rescue him. Only no one would come until over 24 hours later, and by then it was too late.

His eyes were closed, and there was a stream of dried blood that ran from his mouth and pooled underneath his head. His shirt was raised to just below his chest and exposed several of the wounds to his side and stomach. The trunk of the car was completely dark when closed, of course, and it appeared Bailey had tried to feel the severity of the attack on his body. He would have run his hands over every stab wound to his stomach and chest, wincing in pain as he touched each one. There was also a bleeding cut above his eye that looked like a gash from a punch or blow to the head. Bailey's hands weren't scratched or bruised, as they would have been if he'd tried to claw or punch his way out. He couldn't have known the keys to his life were in the car's ignition only a few feet away. He was trapped.

Bailey was simply laying there, the dark trunk now a coffin. It was like he had been buried alive.

The police had found Coach Bailey, but where was Coach Reagor? The two were last seen together, and the police were wondering if Reagor had met with the same fate as Bailey.

Tulsa Tribune Newspaper photographer Don Hayden arrived and immediately began taking photographs of the house, the car and the crime scene. Hayden's flash couldn't recycle fast enough as he took picture after picture. The car, the house, the weeds, the trunk, the body, and the blood were all photographed. He was the first of the print media to arrive, and he was going to take as many pictures as he could, using all of his film. After all, all of the news media, print, radio and television, were covering this story, and Hayden had gotten there first.

The Tulsa Tribune, known as the other Tulsa newspaper, was a rival to the Tulsa World, but the World was still seen as the top newspaper in the area.

The car and the photographer were surrounded by police, who constantly told Hayden to get back from the crime scene. He obliged, but things got tense when the police demanded his film. An unidentified police officer approached Hayden and told him to relinquish the film that he had just shot. Hayden refused, and the two engaged in a verbal altercation. Hayden told him that he would destroy the film himself before giving it up to anyone other than his editor.

There's a saying in news photography: If a man is drowning and you could help him or take the shot, the only question to ask yourself is, "what speed film do I use?"

At the time, some police officers would take photographs of traffic accidents or crime scenes and sell them to attorneys, insurance companies and newspapers for a nice fee. That's no longer accepted. Bob Sherrill, who was a crime reporter at the Sapulpa Herald, starting in the mid-1990s, was once arrested by an Oklahoma Highway Patrol officer for photographing an accident and eventually won a lawsuit against the state of Oklahoma. Sherrill would never divulge how much he was awarded, but he didn't have to work after that. He chose to.

Tribune head photographer Royce Craig then arrived on the scene and retrieved Hayden's film to take back to the paper. The pictures ran in the Tulsa Tribune newspaper the next day.

While the deputies were investigating the car, helicopter pilot Steve McKim asked if he could check out the house and was granted permission. Ed Poston, the TV reporter, decided to stay outside of the house because he wasn't armed and felt uncomfortable about the search. He saw what happened to Bailey and wasn't about to walk into a situation where he might have to defend himself without a weapon.

The helicopter pilot carefully walked into the house, looking into each room. He walked slowly and carefully as the wooden floors creaked with every step. Using caution, he stuck his head inside the doorway of the bedrooms. He wanted to be as careful as he could. The abandoned house was eerily quiet, but he could hear the muffled voices of the officers talking outside by the car. He could also hear the wind whipping around the house, making the search even creepier. The house had a musty odor, and the air was thick with dust. The farmhouse had been abandoned for years but was now over run with intruders, searching for answers.

McKim would peer through the crack between the door and the frame before sticking his head all the way into the room. He felt a sense of relief when it was empty. The creaking noise from the old door hinges was like something out of a horror movie, and the tension was as thick as the air. With each step, the pilot disturbed the thick layer of dust on the floor, making it even harder for him to breath. The creaking sound seemed louder and louder with every room searched.

McKim reached the end of the hall and was standing in front of the only room in the house he hadn't searched. If anyone was in the house, they would be in this room. He stood in front of the bedroom door in the northwest portion of the house and slowly turned the door knob, looking through the opening with caution. He saw a figure lying on the floor and immediately closed the door for his safety. McKim then rushed outside to notify the deputies of his find.

"There's a guy inside laying on a mattress. I think he's mumbling. I saw blood on him. He's in there. He's alive," McKim said excitedly pointing at the house.

Police officers did not know if the figure in the room was the killer, the missing coach or a bum looking for shelter. With guns drawn, every officer crept into the house and walked towards the room located in the northwest corner.

"Police Department!"

"Police Department!"

"Is there anyone in the house? Police Department," was shouted by several different officers as they checked each room with their guns raised about chest-high.

They crept towards the room where McKim said the man was located. The door was pushed opened by an officer and the others rushed inside. They noticed a black male, fitting the other coach's description covered in blood, lying on a burned mattress in an otherwise empty bedroom. The search was over. They found the other missing coach, Paul Reagor Jr.

The black male was laying on his right side covered in blood, sprawled out on half of the mattress in apparent shock and mumbling incoherently.

The officers had to make sure the house was clear and searched every room, but did not find anyone else in the house, which was no longer quiet.

Other than Reagor and the burned mattress, the room was empty. It was relatively small at about 10-feet by 12-feet and didn't have any furnishings. The room had hardwood floors, and the walls were covered in floral wallpaper, giving the house the feeling of a once warm and tranquil dwelling. But, in an instance, it had turned into a grizzly crime scene. There was a stale smell in the air and a hint of a burned odor, omitting from the mattress, which had apparently been torched long before Reagor ended up on it.

The dazed man was wearing dark blue dress pants with a black leather belt, a beige colored light-wool jacket, a white button-up dress shirt with a white T-shirt underneath. They were the same clothes he had been wearing Thursday morning when he was last seen at the school.

It was around noon on Friday, and the teachers had been missing for just over 24 hours.

Reagor's dress and under shirts were covered in blood, and he was in obvious need of medical attention. There was enough blood on him for a serious injury, but not enough for him to be near death.

He was lying on the mattress with his eyes open, and he was breathing heavily. His head remained stationary looking at the ceiling as if he was paralyzed, but his eyes followed the movement in the room.

McKim, who had followed behind the officers, asked Reagor if he could get up and walk on his own, but there was no response. He asked several other questions, but they were met with a blank stare. The police had to get Reagor out of the room so medics could work on him, but it was becoming obvious that he was not going to move on his own. The medics needed more room to assess his wounds, and the police officers needed to ask him questions, but the coach was not assisting to make either possible.

OHP Trooper Thomsen and Officer Robert Broome, with the assistance of McKim and his crew decided to move Reagor into the kitchen area so the officers could check him and the mattress for weapons. None were found, but a can of "Gym Finish" floor cleaner was located near Reagor. The can was apparently punctured with, what was thought to be a screwdriver, but no screwdriver was found. No screwdriver was ever found.

As law enforcement began to work the crime scene, it started to look like Reagor wasn't a victim, but a suspect. He was covered in blood but they couldn't find any stab wounds. The officers raised Reagor's shirt and looked at his stomach and his back but couldn't find any injuries. They looked at his arms and legs but nothing was found other than a few cuts on his hands. Reagor wasn't hurt and Bailey's dead body was found in his trunk. He became the first and only suspect.

Some police officers suspected the floor cleaner had been used by Reagor as an inhalant and a screwdriver and a gun were beginning to look like the murder weapons, but they couldn't find either.

After placing Reagor in the kitchen area, Johnson and several other officers checked the room to make sure there wasn't anything else they had missed. Thomsen and the rest of the officers had originally thought that both Bailey and Reagor had been shot by a small caliber handgun or riffle due to the size of Bailey's injuries and the amount of blood on Reagor's body.

Reagor was again checked for injuries, but none were found. The only blood on Reagor's shirt hadn't come from any trauma to his own body. It became apparent that he was covered in someone else's blood -- Jerry Bailey's blood.

Trooper Thomsen wondered if it was possible that Bailey and Reagor were attacked by a third party, and Reagor fought off the assailant after Bailey was killed. It was a long shot but a possibility. Everything had to be considered. The officers couldn't jump to conclusions but they needed to be realistic. If the two coaches were attacked, why was Bailey's body in Reagor's trunk? Why didn't Reagor call the police? Why didn't Reagor try to help Bailey?

That scenario was unlikely. Reagor was again the top suspect, but he wasn't talking. Not yet.

The kitchen floor's checkered tile was covered with an inch or two of dirt and grime, with trash and shards of glass scattered everywhere from the room's broken windows. Since the house had been abandoned for some time, the windows were probably broken by area kids that threw rocks at the house on a dare or out of boredom. There were now dusty footprints all over the inside of the house. The officer's boot prints were scattered from the bed room in the northwest corner to the kitchen to the front door. The once thick air was now much thinner due to all of the excitement, and the front door stayed open because of all of the traffic in and out.

McKim started asking Reagor questions, again.

"Sir, are you injured?"

No response.

"Sir, can you hear me? Where have you been hurt? Were you stabbed?"

No response.

"Can you hear me? Can you answer my questions?"

No response.

"Are you hurt? Answer me. I need you to talk to me. I can't help you if you don't tell me where you are injured."

None of McKim's questions were answered by Reagor, who laid there like a zombie, staring at the dirty, cracked ceiling.

At 12:30 p.m., Tulsa County Lt. Deputy Sheriff Bob Randolph arrived at the scene and immediately took charge of the investigation. The Tulsa County Sheriff's Office was now in charge.

Randolph was a tall, 47-year old, handsome man with a stocky build and a full head of brown hair that was receding just a bit, giving him a slight widow's peak. He was clean-shaven with sideburns that were grown below his ears, nearing his square jawline. Randolph wore business suits instead of a sheriff's deputy uniform, and, on this day, he chose a solid color suit coat with pattern tie and checkered pants with dress shoes.

Randolph was from Hanson, Oklahoma, which no longer exists. It was located near Sallisaw, but closer to Fort Smith, Ark. The town of Hanson was buried under the Arkansas River when the river was diverted.

He attended Hanson Public Schools growing up and was a veteran of the armed forces, having served in the U.S. Air Force. He was married with two children, and spent his career as a deputy sheriff for the Tulsa County Sheriff's Office. He was involved in the Sertoma Club, was a 32nd degree Mason and a dual member of Tulsa and Owasso Masonic Lodge. He lived in Owasso, Oklahoma at the time of the murder.

Even though Sapulpa police were there, the crime scene was located in Tulsa County, a few miles away from Creek County. At this point, no one knew where Bailey was actually murdered, but the body was found in Bixby, and Randolph was now the lead investigator. This was his crime scene now.

Randolph received a call from the dispatcher at noon and was informed that the car they had been looking for had been found and that Bailey's body was in the trunk. Around the same time, a call was made to Sapulpa High School to inform the administration that the two coaches were found and that Bailey was dead. John Cockrum was the business administrator at Sapulpa High School, but was the high school principal before getting the new job. He was in on the hiring of Bailey five years before and got to know the Bailey family very well.

The Sapulpa city manager also called Cockrum at the administration building and informed him of Bailey's death.

"Are you sure?" Cockrum said, wanting a different answer.

"Yes," the city manager said, "The Police Chief is here, and he confirmed that it's Jerry's body."

Word was getting out, and Cockrum needed to get to Beverly, Guy and Diedra before anyone else did, especially the press. The Sapulpa Daily Herald had been on top of the story since the coaches went missing that Thursday morning. Cockrum hung up the phone and immediately rushed to his car. He had to tell Beverly in person. Cockrum turned out of the parking lot and headed south on Mission Street towards the Bailey house, which was located in the Tanglewood addition. The drive was very familiar to him; he lived only a few houses down from the Bailey's, but this was a drive he wished he didn't have to make.

As he drove down Mission Street, he remembered hiring Bailey from Nowata High School, which is located about 70 miles from Sapulpa. Cockrum, who was the school's principal at that time, along with school superintendent Joe Martin and several school board members, made the one-and-a-half hour drive to Nowata to hire Bailey just five years before, and now, he had to drive to Bailey's house to tell his wife that her husband was dead. He also remembered the rumors about Reagor being upset with Bailey, but it was just a rumor -- until now. Cockrum's mind was racing. He was trying to put the pieces together of what happened and why, but nothing made sense.

Cockrum had just been hired as a school administrator, and this really didn't fall under his job duties, but the Baileys were like family to him. He pulled into the driveway, put his car in park and sat there for a second with the engine off. He was trying to think of what to say and how to say it, but the words weren't coming to him. He didn't want to wait any longer and quickly got out of the car. He stopped for a moment, exhaled and walked up the steps to the front door. He knocked and was greeted by the pastor of the First Baptist Church, the Reverend John W.

Cook, who could see by the look on Cockrum's face that he was bringing devastating news.

Reverend Cook had been pacing in the living room, but Beverly was upstairs in her bedroom, praying to God that her husband would come home alive. Cook had spent the morning talking and praying with Beverly, attempting to get her mind off of what was going on, but she eventually retired to her room. A room she shared with Jerry. She needed to talk to God by herself.

"Where's Beverly?" Cockrum asked with the corners of his mouth turned down.

"She's upstairs, John," Cook said, placing his hand on Cockrum's shoulder.

"You'd better go with me," Cockrum said with sadness in his voice.

Reverend Cook didn't have to ask why. His body had been tense all morning, but as soon as he saw Cockrum, his shoulders sunk, and he slowly bowed his head to the side. He knew Bailey was dead, and he knew he had to be a rock for Beverly and the children. Cook followed Cockrum up the stairs to the master bedroom. Cockrum was still trying to figure out how to tell Beverly her husband was dead. He could have told her a million different ways but he decided to just tell her as quickly as he could. She deserved to know as soon as possible.

Beverly was sitting on her bed and was visibly shaken. Cockrum entered the room and their eyes met. He could see she already knew the truth, but he knew he still had to tell her. He sat down beside her on the bed and put his hands on top of hers. Her hands were in her lap, and she was clutching and pulling at a Kleenex that had long lost its usefulness. He cocked his head to the side, took a breath, and the words started to come out -- words he didn't want to say.

He swallowed the lump in his throat and said, "Beverly, they found Jerry, and he's dead."

Beverly began to sob and slumped into Cockrum's arms. He didn't say anything more. There was nothing more to say. After a few moments of comforting Beverly, Cockrum motioned for Cook to take care of the distraught widow. Cockrum was fighting back tears, but he had a job to do and owed it to the Bailey family. He knew the newspaper and television media were converging on the school, and he had to get back to the administration building to do his job.

Guy and Diedra were at the house, and Beverly didn't want anyone else to tell them about their father's death -- she had to do it. Beverly and Reverend Cook took the kids to their bedrooms and shut the door. The house then filled with school administrators, police officers and friends.

Back at the school, Shibley was sitting at the scorer's table in the gymnasium getting ready for the wrestling tournament, but his missing friend weighed heavily on his mind. The matches were about to begin when Sapulpa High School Principal Charles Dodson walked into the gym. Shibley readied himself to stand firm that the tournament would go on, that they wouldn't repeat the morning's argument.

But Dodson didn't come to talk about the tournament. He leaned in to whisper in the coach's ear. Dodson didn't want any of the students around the table to hear what he was about to say. "They found Jerry, and he's dead."

The words echoed in Shibley's head, and everything started moving in slow-motion. Shibley slumped down into his chair and sat stunned. A lump formed in his throat. He wanted to ask a million questions, but all he could manage to say was, "Oh my God."

An announcement was made over the high school intercom that the coaches had been found and that Bailey was dead. The Sapulpa wrestling tournament was in full swing, and the high school gym was full of students who paid fifty cents to get out of class and watch their friends wrestle. By then, parents had already heard the news and some were coming up to the school to tell their kids in person. Terry Holbrook, who saw the two coaches that Thursday morning, saw his dad, Bobby Holbrook, outside of the doors to the gym, and he pointed to his son to join him out in the hall. Holbrook, a sophomore, started walking down the stairs and had a feeling he knew what his dad was going to tell him. Rumors were already circulating in the gym about Bailey's death, and once Holbrook joined his dad in the hallway, he was told what he already knew in his heart.

With tears in his eyes, Holbrook walked back into the gym and saw several football players walking down the stairs to the old wrestling room located under the gym floor. The old wrestling room was now storage for the old wrestling mats. It was an old locker room turned into a storage room where old desks and furniture went to decompose. The room also doubled as a fallout shelter and, eventually, a storm shelter. There were still wooden benches in front of the lockers and the football team had assembled down there to get away from the other students.

Not a single word was spoken, and the only sound that could be heard was crying. All of the football players were shedding tears over their slain coach.

The tournament, which started two hours late, was finally canceled at Sapulpa, and the Friday afternoon and Saturday matches were transferred to the Ed Dubie Field House at Sand Springs. Sapulpa High School also canceled classes for the remainder of the day, Friday.

Back at the crime scene, reporters from television news stations, newspapers and radio converged on the farmhouse, and it was starting to get cramped. Nearly 20 reporters were standing around with cameras, notepads and microphones, waiting to get just a sliver of information to start their story. By 2:30 p.m., two hours after the coaches were found, Lt. Randolph held an impromptu press

48

conference, but it was more about getting the press out of his way rather than giving them information. He gave the newsmen all of the details that he wanted to be released at the moment, keeping several things close to the vest so it wouldn't hinder the investigation. After he answered a few questions, the reporters ran back to their cars and sped away from the scene in order to get back to their desks to write up the story about how the missing persons investigation turned into a murder investigation.

In the weekend edition of the Sapulpa Daily Herald Newspaper, sports editor Terry Goggin wrote an editorial titled "He Was Their Friend" in which he pointed out Bailey's generosity and camaraderie with his players and coaches. Goggin wrote:

"They wept Friday at Sapulpa High. Mute coaches and teachers with swollen eyes tried vainly to go about their business. A young girl sat on the front school lawn in the bright sunshine, her face in her hands. Athletes were stunned. Wrestler and football player Don Christensen was one of the majority to stay and compete in the weekend's wrestling tournament. 'Coach Bailey would have wanted us to stay,' a distraught Christensen said. Other wrestlers agreed."

Goggin wrote how race relations improved at Sapulpa under Bailey's steady hand, and his calm but intense presence served to smooth over differences which could have mushroomed into genuine problems.

Assistant football coach Johnny "Smoke" Richardson added how confusing and puzzling the situation was for everyone. "There was a lot of respect between Jerry and Paul," said a shaken Richardson. "They had never had an argument. Never."

CHAPTER FOUR
PAUL REAGOR JR.

Paul Reagor Jr. was born April 30, 1943 to Paul Reagor Sr. and Obzinder Reagor. He was the fourth of six children and he had three brothers, Willie, James and John, and two sisters, Rose and Delores.

He was born and raised in Okmulgee, Oklahoma in an atmosphere that stressed traditional values and attributes concerning productivity, responsibility, moral behavior and self-improvement through education. The family was also very religious and stressed the importance of moral character.

All six children began working at an early age and all were educated past the high school level. Their vocation ranged from teacher to industrial plant supervisor to beautician. Their parents also stressed the importance of abiding by the law and upholding certain principles. None had a criminal record.

During their childhood, all of the children were encouraged to excel and improve their place in life through hard work, knowledge and dedication. The children maintained a "poor but proud" attitude and pushed each other to achieve their goals. The kids picked cotton at a young age and combined their money to send each other to college or vocational school.

The family unit was close and always looked out for one another.

Obzinder Reagor was a loving mother and displayed moral support for all of her children. She described her son Paul Jr. as a quiet introspective and cooperative child who retained the same characteristics in his adult life as well as motivation toward educational enrichment, professional dedication and humanitarian concern for others.

Paul Reagor Jr. attended Dunbar High School – a predominately black school -- in Okmulgee (it later integrated into Okmulgee High School) and graduated in

1961 while maintaining a high grade-point average. During his high school career at Dunbar, he was the starting quarterback and captain of the football team, while being president of his senior class.

After his graduation in 1961, he attended Langston University and played football all four years. He was captain of the football team his senior year and again senior class president. Reagor was a member of the Alpha Phi Alpha Fraternity, the Student Teachers Association, and the Student Government Association. He graduated college in 1965 with a Bachelor's Degree of Arts in Education, and by 1970, he had completed 38 hours towards his Master's Degree and maintained a high GPA.

After graduating college, Reagor was employed by his alma mater Dunbar High School in 1965. He was then hired by Okmulgee High School as a history teacher and an assistant coach in multiple sports when the Dunbar and Okmulgee schools were consolidated due to desegregation in 1969. At Okmulgee, he was an assistant football, basketball and track coach and was instrumental in helping the two schools transition into one.

He also worked with the school's multiracial Human Relations Committee, and the group was a major factor in the implementing the desegregation of the schools, which had a 40 percent minority population. The effective function of the group was due to Reagor, and he also doubled as a counselor in regards to racially-charge situations.

He was then promoted to assistant principal at Okmulgee during the 1974-75 school year before accepting the job at Sapulpa High School in August of 1975. Reagor was named Assistant Principal in charge of attendance, and an assistant coach under then four-year head coach Jerry Bailey.

It has been widely speculated that the Sapulpa school administration brought Reagor in to help discipline the black students and to help with the racial tension that had been plaguing the high school since its integration in 1960. Reagor was also a good football coach, and Jerry Bailey always surrounded himself with a staff that was capable of coaching championship teams.

CHAPTER FIVE
The investigation

Tulsa County Lt. Bob Randolph took the keys to Reagor's car and opened the trunk to see Jerry Bailey's body for himself. Randolph had been on the force for many years and had seen more than his share of dead bodies, and this one was no different to him. He scanned the body for obvious injuries and saw what he thought was a gunshot wound just above the belt line. He thought there had to be a gun somewhere.

Randolph closed the trunk of the car to preserve the crime scene and headed back into the farmhouse. By now, uniformed officers from several different precincts were gathering around the house. Officers from Sapulpa, Bixby, Tulsa, and the highway patrol were standing guard to preserve the crime scene, but some were there because they wanted to know what happened to their friend.

Paul Reagor was still lying on the floor of the kitchen. Now, even more medical personnel started asking questions, trying to determine if he was injured.

"Sir, are you alright?"

"Sir, where are you injured? Where are you bleeding from? What happened? Are you in any pain?"

"Talk to me, sir. I can't help you unless you tell us what's going on."

But he remained still and silent now with his eyes closed. Randolph was more concerned about placing his only suspect under arrest.

"Paul Reagor?" Randolph asked loudly with a harshness to his voice. The coach opened his eyes in response.

"You have the right to remain silent...," the officer rattled off the Miranda Rights, but Reagor didn't seem to listen. He had heard these rights time after time due to television and movies, but this time the police were talking to him.

"Do you understand your rights?"

"Yes," Reagor answered, staring at the ceiling. This was the first time Reagor had uttered a word. He was finally talking, and maybe now police officers would get some answers.

"Why did you shoot Jerry Bailey?"

"What?" Reagor said, confused.

"Where's the gun?"

"What gun?" Reagor asked.

The medics began taking Reagor's pulse and checking his blood pressure, asking Reagor if he felt any pain. He didn't even flinch when the cold steel of the stethoscope touched his bare chest. The ripping sound of the Velcro on the blood pressure cuff, which almost didn't fit around Reagor's large bicep muscle, sounded louder in the empty house and broke Randolph's concentration, stopping the questioning for a second.

The police again assessed his wounds and were puzzled at the amount of blood on his clothing. The medics slid him onto a stretcher, secured him with restraints, and locked the gurney into position. Randolph stepped back, waiting for the medical personnel to finish their tasks before he continued. Sapulpa Officer Richard Johnson placed handcuffs around Reagor's wrists, tightening them because of the man's huge hands. Victims weren't generally handcuffed while on a stretcher, but it became clear that Reagor wasn't a victim. He was an assailant, and he was read his Miranda Rights.

The medics brought Reagor out of the house and onto the front porch. The planks on the porch were uneven and partially rotten, forcing the medics to lift the stretcher, relieving some of the weight on the unstable porch. The medics strained and several officers helped lift the stretcher. Reagor squinted as the sun hit his face for the first time since he walked into the house over 24 hours earlier. The police officers that were outside, collecting evidence and securing the crime scene by the car stopped what they were doing. They followed the gurney with their eyes as the medics tried to maneuver it across the yard over the dead grass, gravel and rocks. They had to see the man that killed his friend and stuffed him into a dirty trunk to die.

The medics loaded the stretcher into the back of a Broken Arrow ambulance. Randolph asked Officer Johnson to ride with the suspect to the hospital, and Johnson obliged, climbing inside the vehicle before the heavy back door slammed shut. The officer was supposed to monitor Reagor on his way to the hospital, but that didn't mean he couldn't talk to him. Johnson wanted to know what happened.

Randolph stayed behind to secure the crime scene and talk to the medical examiner, Dr. Robert Fogel, who arrived soon after to oversee the removal of Bailey's body from the trunk of the car.

With red lights flashing and sirens blaring, the ambulance headed for Hillcrest Hospital, just east of downtown Tulsa, a 15-minute ride from the farmhouse. Johnson sat on the bench to the left of Reagor's stretcher. Hardly a novice, Johnson had been a member of the Sapulpa Police Department for seven years. A graduate of Tulsa Junior College and Northeastern State University, Johnson had studied criminal justice and investigations before completing the Military Police Academy. During his seven years on the force, Johnson had investigated an average of five to six homicides a year and was no stranger to protocol and proper procedure. He noticed small cuts on Reagor's hands that were still slightly bleeding, cuts that couldn't have produced the blood that was on Reagor's shirts. The suspect was covered in blood, and the cuts on his hands were small as if he had cut them with a small knife.

"Mr. Reagor, I'm Officer Johnson from the Sapulpa Police Department."

Reagor interrupted Johnson and answered before being asked a question. "I guess what I did was wrong."

"What do you mean by that?"

"What I did to Jerry," Reagor said.

Reagor's voice was hoarse from being inside an abandoned farmhouse on a cold winter's night. He hadn't had anything to eat or drink and was probably dehydrated. His voice was shaky and he spoke slightly above a whisper. Reagor's body shook from the cold, making the handcuffs clank on the buckle of the restraints. Johnson had to hold on to a handle attached to the roof of the ambulance, forcing him to occasionally lean over the suspect during the bumpy ride to the hospital.

"What did you do to Jerry?" Johnson asked.

"I hurt him," Reagor said looking directly at the officer.

"How did you hurt him?"

"I stabbed him."

Johnson was confused. Randolph had said there was a gunshot wound on the body.

"Don't you mean shot him?"

"No, I stabbed him," Reagor said.

"Where did you stab Jerry?"

Reagor looked away from the officer and gazed at the roof of the ambulance, as if trying to replay the murder in his mind.

"It was off to the side of the road. I don't remember, but it was off of Mingo road."

"What did you do after you stabbed him?"

"I stabbed him with a knife, and I put him in the trunk and drove around for a while."

Johnson was a little confused. He had seen what he thought was a gunshot wound, but Reagor was talking, and he wasn't going to stop him. He went through the checklist of questions. "What did you do with the knife after you stabbed Jerry?"

"I threw it out down the road."

"How long were you at the house?"

"I don't know."

"Why did you stab Jerry?"

Reagor was silent for a moment: "I guess it was because of the hate."

The answer puzzled the officer. Johnson knew that Bailey and Reagor were friends, and from the briefings the day before, Bailey had likely gone willingly with Reagor. What had gone on in those final hours away from the school? Was there something upsetting Reagor that even Jerry Bailey hadn't known?

By 1 p.m. the ambulance reached the Hillcrest Hospital emergency room in Tulsa. Reagor's stretcher was unloaded and wheeled into the ER. Nurses and doctors stared at the man on the stretcher. They had been warned a murder suspect was coming in to be treated, and this was the man who allegedly killed a fellow football coach. It was all over the news, and now the medical staff was part of one of the biggest stories to hit Oklahoma in years. Patients sitting in the ER waiting room also stared. They didn't know who the man was on the stretcher, but he was accompanied by a police officer. It was interesting to those in the waiting room, to say the least, and it got a lot more interesting when more and more police officers and detectives started arriving at the hospital, looking for the man on the stretcher.

Reagor was immediately whisked into one of the tiny emergency room stalls. Officer Johnson took the key from his belt and removed Reagor's handcuffs so the doctors and nurses could work on the suspect without any hindrance. But Johnson was a bit reluctant and was never more than a few feet away from his suspect. The medical staff would just have to work around him. Reagor had just admitted to the murder of a friend for no apparent reason.

While the medical staff began its work on Reagor, Johnson saw Tulsa County Deputy Sheriff Norman Whisenhunt and officially turned over the murder suspect to him. The case was now in the hands of Tulsa County. Bixby was located in Tulsa County and as bad as the Sapulpa Police Department wanted to handle the investigation, the crime didn't occur in their jurisdiction – the city of Sapulpa or Creek County. Reagor admitted to Johnson he killed Bailey on Mingo road, which is located in Bixby.

Whisenhunt had been assigned to guard Reagor at the hospital. Johnson told Whisenhunt about Reagor's incriminating statements in the ambulance and that Deputy Randolph had read Reagor his rights at the crime scene. Reagor affirmed that he understood his rights.

Whisenhunt walked into the exam room. He made a visual assessment of the suspect and was impressed with Reagor's size. Whisenhunt began asking the suspect questions.

"Mr. Reagor, have you been advised of your Miranda Rights?"

Reagor nodded his head.

"And you understand those rights?"

Reagor again replied in the affirmative with a nod. For the second time, Reagor acknowledged that he understood his rights.

The deputy moved to the foot of Reagor's hospital bed. He reached into his suit coat pocket and pulled out his notebook and pen. He wanted to write everything down and have a record of what Reagor was about to tell him. He clicked the top of the pen and placed it onto the first line of the note pad. He was ready.

"What happened in the two days you two were missing?"

The nurses continued their work, and Reagor struggled to speak. He told Whisenhunt about meeting Jerry in the school parking lot on Thursday morning.

"We drove around, and then I told him I wanted to show him something in the trunk of the car. We pulled over, and I handed him the keys, and he walked around the car to the trunk." Reagor cleared his throat and sniffed loudly. "I got a butcher knife I had put under the seat several days earlier."

Reagor had now admitted that the murder was premeditated and not a random act or self-defense. The murder of Jerry Bailey was planned and deliberate.

Officer Johnson had told Deputy Whisenhunt that detectives were looking for the murder weapon, and the gun Reagor had used to shoot Bailey hadn't been recovered. Now, Whisenhunt wondered whether there was even a gun at all. But Reagor was offering a lot of details, so Whisenhunt decided not to ask about the gun, allowing Reagor continue with the details of the murder. He knew if a murder suspect was going to keep talking he had better not stop him.

Reagor just admitted to stabbing Bailey with a butcher knife he had taken from his own kitchen at home. Why would he lie about the murder weapon? There was no gun.

Reagor continued, "I told him, 'You're the one that's been messing me around,' and he said, 'You've got the wrong guy. I haven't been messing you around.' Then I started stabbing him, and I put his body in the trunk."

Messing him around about what, the deputy wondered? He wrote the phrase "messing me around" on his notepad, and his pen made a scratching noise as he underlined the phrase twice. The medical staff had stabilized Reagor but had held back on any invasive tests while the suspect was being questioned.

Several hours later, at around 3 p.m., Officer Bob Randolph arrived at the hospital. He went into Reagor's emergency room stall and began talking with the suspect. A bevy of doctors and nurses were in and out of the small room attending to Reagor. Dr. Lawrence Reed was the attending physician, and several nurses, including emergency room technician Emma Gray, assisted with Reagor's care. The nurses had difficulty removing Reagor's clothes because he refused to help the medical staff and just sat there, listless, looking off into space. The suspect sat on the edge of the hospital bed with his feet resting on a metal stool. Tiny white globs of dried spit had formed in the corners of Reagor's mouth.

Reagor still spoke just slightly above a whisper, and it was obvious his mouth was dry. He hadn't had a drink the entire time he was in the farmhouse, and he was dehydrated. The nurses started an IV drip of fluids and electrolytes to help rehydrate his body after over 24 hours without water.

"Do you remember me?" Randolph asked.

"Yes."

"Do you remember being advised of your rights?"

"Yes."

"Did you kill Jerry Bailey?" Randolph said.

"Yes," Reagor said, without hesitation.

"Why?"

"Because he was messing me around."

Messing him around, Randolph wondered?

"What did you kill him with?" the detective asked.

"A butcher knife."

"How many times did you stab him?"

Reagor took a breath and exhaled, "More than once."

"Where's the butcher knife now?"

"I threw it out the window when I was driving. I don't remember where, but it was down the road on Mingo." Reagor said.

While Randolph was interrogating Reagor, the suspect's fingernails were scraped and the material was placed in a clear evidence bag, and his bloody clothes were removed and placed in a large brown paper sack. An ER technician wrote "REAGOR" on the sack with a black magic marker. It was now evidence.

Once the examination was completed, Reagor was moved to the mental ward of the hospital, Two North.

Then Mr. Reagor's attorney, Jim Goodwin entered the room and watched the questioning. He didn't say a word or ask the police officers to stop asking questions. He just watched as if he was a spectator. He looked on while his client confessed to pre-meditated murder. The attorney was present because Dr. Lawrence Reed called him by request of the Reagor family that had already assembled in the hospital waiting room.

The Sapulpa Daily Herald heard of the news and held the publication of the paper Friday morning until it could obtain more details and release a story. The newspaper was printed in the morning and distributed in the early afternoon, but the editor waited until he could confirm Bailey's death and Reagor's apprehension.

Coach Bailey Is Slain; Reagor Held In Custody

The body of Jerry Bailey, who resigned as Sapulpa high school football coach last month was found in the trunk of a car in Tulsa County shortly before noon Friday, and SHS Vice Principal Paul Reagor Jr. was found lying incoherently on the floor of a nearby abandoned farm house.

Bailey, 35,(he was actually 34) *and Reagor, 33, had been missing since Thursday when they were last seen leaving the Sapulpa school parking lot at 8:15 a.m.*

Blood-spattered personal papers belonging to Bailey were found by Bixby Police about two hours later, and a search was begun.

Sapulpa detectives Tom Clark and Joe Collins said Reagor was covered with blood and in a state of shock but

61

appeared to have no external wounds. He was under guard in a Tulsa hospital.

Bailey's body had a bullet hole in the right side above the belt, and several other wounds. It was in the trunk of Reagor's car which was spotted at 11:30 a.m. near 145th E. Ave and 131st St. by a Medivac-Helicopter ambulance. The car was about 90 yards from the house. The scene is about five miles east of Bixby, in far south Broken Arrow.

Officers started their hunt for the pair when Bixby Police called Sapulpa Police at mid-morning on Thursday, saying Bailey's papers with fresh blood on them had been found by citizens on Mingo Road between 121st St. and 131st St.

Bailey of 1024 E. Courtney, resigned on Dec. 8 as head football coach after five seasons...

When the Herald published the story, a gun was still suspected as the murder weapon.

The local newspaper established the Jerry Bailey Memorial Fund the day after the coaches were found. The fund was set up to provide money for the principal purpose of providing an educational trust for the Bailey children, Guy and Diedra. Immediately, funds started pouring in from all over the state. The newspaper printed the names of everyone that contributed money, and in just three days, $3,000 was collected. Contributions were large and small, from children, adults, families and businesses. Several families from Nowata sent money in reverence for their former coach, teacher and friend. The final contributions totaled around $20,000. The Nowata Daily Star also set up a fund that would be used for the Bailey children's education.

Reagor spent the beginning of the week at the hospital but was taken to the court house for his preliminary hearing on Thursday, January 29, 1976 in front of Associate District Judge Bill Beasley.

The defendant attended the hearing strapped to a stretcher and refused to enter a plea. The court entered a plea of "not guilty" on his behalf, and his attorney and the district attorney filed an application for order of mental observation at a psychiatric hospital. Reagor was now represented by Tulsa attorney Don Gasaway, and the joint-request was filed by Gasaway and Tulsa County Chief Prosecutor Ron Shaffer.

CHAPTER SIX
The Medical Examiner

Medical Examiner, Robert Fogel, arrived on the scene and started filling out the paperwork for the initial investigation report. This was the biggest case in the state and it would soon receive national attention. Everything had to be done by the book. The paperwork had to be filled out correctly and there wasn't much mystery surrounding the death of Jerry Bailey. At least not from a medical stand point. Standing in the middle of the crime scene, Fogel started writing on his clipboard.

The usual information was recorded:

Name: Jerry Bailey
Age: 33 (he was 34)
Race: White
Sex: Male
Marital status: Married
Address: 1024 E. Courtney, Sapulpa, OK
Occupation: Football Coach

Under the Type of Death section, the box labeled "violent, unusual or unnatural means" was marked, and that seemed to be an understatement. Fogel noted that rigor mortis, which is the stiffening of the joints and muscles a few hours after death, had started to set in. This usually lasted from one to four days. Blood was also leaking from Bailey's mouth.

Manner of death: Homicide.

Fogel had finished his initial report at the crime scene, but he still had work to do back at the office. The M.E. now had to find out how many times Bailey had been stabbed and which of the wounds led to his death. He knew this wasn't going to be an easy task. Most of Fogel's autopsy's involved a bullet wound or two, and stabbing victims usually never had more than three or four stabs in a concentrated area. This was going to take a while, and he knew he had his work cut out for him. The autopsy wasn't performed until around noon, Saturday, January 24, 1976 in the Tulsa County Morgue, 48 hours after the murder.

The Autopsy Report - Autopsy # T-21-76

Postmortem injuries: *Deceased has been in the morgue cooler. Laceration left lateral upper lip with abrasion, 1/4 inch by 3/16 of an inch. Laceration, left lateral lower lip, 1/8 inch in diameter. Laceration, left ear, 3-8 of an inch by 1/4 inch. Extensive blood stains, chest, abdomen, upper extremities-most prominent hands, palmer surface. Abrasion right anterior chest.

Pathological Diagnosis

1. Penetrating stab wound (one) left suburicular region with extension into left carotid sheath with hematoma left carotid sheath.

2. Penetrating stab wounds, anterior chest (two), with associated hematoma, mediastinum.

3. Penetrating stab wounds, left posterolateral neck (one).

4. Penetrating stab wounds, left shoulder (three), with envolvment of left thoracic inlet.

5. Penetrating stab wounds, upper dorsal region (two).

6. Penetrating stab wounds, lower dorsal region (five), with envolvment of right lung, right hemidiaphram, and superior right lobe, liver.

7. Penetrating stab wounds (six), lumbar and sacral regions with right perenial hematoma.

8. Coronary atherosclerosis, moderate, with cardiomyopathy.

9. Penetrating stab wound (one), anterior abdominal wall, with penetration of mesenteric stalk.

Cause of death: Multiple stab wounds, left-subauricular region, anterior chest, upper anterior abdominal wall, cervical, dorsal, lumbar and sacral regions, with right hemothorax and right pneumothorax with atelectasis.

When Fogel's examination was complete, Jerry Bailey was stabbed 22 times, seven of which could have been, by themselves, fatal. According to the autopsy, Bailey was stabbed in the chest four times which was indicated on the Body Diagram as #1, #2, #3 and #4. He was stabbed in the neck once, #5, and was stabbed in the left shoulder three times, #6, #7 and #8.

A cut below his left ear was labeled #9. The majority of the wounds were to Bailey's back. The upper back and right shoulder were #10, #11, #12, #13, #14, #15 and #16. His lower back, around the right kidney, also had some substantial damage with #17, #18, #19, #20, #21 and #22.

The autopsy revealed that Bailey had died from multiple stab wounds and a massive hemorrhage that filled his right lung. Fogel determined that Bailey had bled to death from his injuries. Injuries that were inflicted by someone filled with rage. The M.E. had seen this before in cases that involved murderers and victims that knew each other on very personal levels. These injuries were driven by anger and hate.

There was no bullet wound, which was originally speculated by police. Bailey had not been shot, and he was not stabbed by a screwdriver, which was a rumor that spread like wildfire.

The lack of defense wounds to the hands and forearms showed that Bailey was probably ambushed from behind and wasn't able to put up much of a fight. Also, Bailey weighed 180-pounds and Reagor weighed 250 pounds. Bailey was outweighed by almost 100-pounds, and at the time of the attack, had no idea that Reagor was angry at him. He had no idea Reagor was angry at all. There was no reason for Bailey to have his guard up or to be prepared for a fight.

It was a surprise attack, and the numerous stab wounds to the back shows that he had no chance of defending himself. But why would he suspect anything? Reagor was a friend, a good friend.

Bailey was said to be "tough as nails." He was a fit and athletic-180 pounds and would sometimes line up across from his defensive line to show his offensive line how to block – without a helmet or shoulder pads. In high school and college, the standout athlete was never on the injured reserve list. He played through his injuries. He also coached wrestling and knew how to use his body. He could have defended himself if he knew he needed to, no matter how big his opponent was.

The coach had a circular wound above his belt line that appeared to be a bullet hole, but the medical examiner determined that it was a stab wound. The knife was plunged into Bailey's body and twisted in a circular motion with such force that it gave the illusion of a bullet hole. Nearly every detective that saw the wound immediately identified it as a bullet wound, and it was leaked to the media that a gun was used to kill Bailey. But that wasn't true.

The police could stop looking for a gun.

The examiner found that the weapon used was probably a standard kitchen knife, and the wounds made a triangle-like pattern. Reagor admitted to police that he used a knife from home. Some of the police detectives speculated that the murder weapon was a screw driver, but Fogel was emphatic the wounds were made by a standard kitchen or paring knife. Doctors speculate that it would have taken Bailey between four and six minutes to die in the trunk of Reagor's car if his lung was filling up with blood. He would have drowned and bled to death, and it wouldn't have taken more than 10 minutes, which would seem like an eternity locked in the trunk of a car.

At first, Police speculated to Bailey's friends that the coach was stabbed several times and then thrown into the trunk. Then, Reagor stopped the car after driving around for a while, opened the trunk and began stabbing him again which might explain the stab wounds to the front and back of Bailey's body. However, Reagor said he threw the knife out of the car while driving down Mingo Road before he stopped at the farmhouse. He wouldn't have had the weapon anymore. All of Bailey's wounds happened during the initial attack, but it is possible that he was stabbed while standing outside of the car and then immediately after he was placed inside the trunk.

The wounds to Bailey's stomach and chest are thought to be the initial wounds because they were the worst of the wounds -- a surprise attack. But it was just speculation, and it happened on the side of a rural road in broad daylight. Not one person witnessed any of it.

DR. NORFLEET

At 6 p.m., on Friday, Jan. 23, Dr. Edward K. Norfleet arrived at Hillcrest Medical Center and made his way to Two North, the mental ward of the hospital. He was asked to examine Reagor and evaluate his mental condition. Since the suspect was generally incoherent and stared off into space, doctors wanted a psychological evaluation. Norfleet had heard about the murder on the radio and was anxious to get started. He didn't know it at the time, but he had become a player in this tragedy a month earlier.

Dr. Norfleet practiced medicine and psychiatry in the Tulsa area and received his undergraduate degree from Baylor University in Waco, Texas. He also earned a degree in chemistry from Johns Hopkins University, in Baltimore, Maryland, and his medical degree from the University of Arkansas, in Little Rock, Arkansas. He did his internships at Crawford Long Hospital in Atlanta, Georgia, and he combined his residencies at the University Hospital, Central State Hospital and in the Veteran's Administration Hospital in Oklahoma City. He also did a residency of psychiatry with additional training outside of the United States in London, England.

Dr. Norfleet was a member of the city, county, and state American Medical Association, the American Psychiatric Association, the Mid-Continent and Southern Psychiatric Association, and the Southern Medical Society.

He was also a member of the psychiatric sections of all of the hospitals in the Tulsa area, and he was the vice-chief of the section at Hillcrest and secretary of St. Francis Hospitals in Tulsa.

However, the day Reagor was brought into the hospital after the coaches were found wouldn't be the first time that Dr. Norfleet had treated him.

On Jan. 9, 1976, thirteen days before the murder, Reagor was taken to Hillcrest Medical Center for a suspected intentional overdose of medication and was admitted for a five-day period due to depression. The overdose was eventually deemed intentional by doctors and marked as an attempted suicide in Reagor's medical chart.

He had taken an overdose of Elavil, an anti-depressant, and Salonex, a nasal spray. Psychiatric nurse Eileen Hollands tended to Reagor during his earlier stay due to the overdose. She looked after him in room 2105 in Two North and described him as, "comatose or on the verge of comatose... No verbalizing at all and he was really out of it."

After the murder, Reagor apparently exhibited the same symptoms as his overdose. The suspect appeared dazed and wouldn't respond to any of the emergency room doctor's questions. The overdose happened two weeks after Reagor was informed he would not be hired as the new football coach at Sapulpa. Art Davis was named as Bailey's successor. Reagor had also missed several days of school the week of the murder and was absent the day before he killed Bailey.

Sapulpa High School Vice Principal Ronald James had tried to contact Reagor several times during his absences, but could only talk to Reagor's wife Emma Jean, a teacher at a Tulsa elementary school. She seemed very evasive and was vague about why her husband was missing so much school. She wouldn't give the actual reason as to why he wasn't there. James felt that she wasn't completely honest with him and didn't find out about the overdose until after the murder.

After Dr. Norfleet's visit, only hours after the two coaches were found, the doctor then saw the suspect on Saturday and Sunday, January 24 and 25, but there was no significant change in his appearance, ability, or willingness to communicate with doctors.

CHAPTER SEVEN
The Funeral

On Monday, January 26, 1976, Jerry Bailey's funeral was held at the First Baptist Church in downtown Sapulpa. Over 1,200 people crammed into two different sanctuaries to attend the funeral of the beloved coach. At Sapulpa, the First Baptist Church is always the most popular church in town. Most of the school's football players attended because the church always had the best parties and cookouts, and the prettiest girls. For years, the First Baptist Church hosted the "Fifth Quarter," a post-football game party that generally welcomed several hundred kids.

In Sapulpa, there isn't a shortage of churches. There seems to be one on every street corner, but when the Bailey's moved from Nowata, they found the First Baptist Church, and it became their church home. Eight hundred people filled the new auditorium, and at least 400 heard the funeral services that were broadcast in the old sanctuary across the street.

A local radio station contacted First Baptist's Reverend Gary W. Cook and told him they wanted to broadcast the funeral on the air. There was no way everyone could get into the funeral to pay their respects, and they wanted to broadcast the funeral on the radio. The station got permission from the school and from the family, and they set up a speaker across the street in the old sanctuary, but the entire town of Sapulpa could also tune in to hear the services. It is said to be the first and only local funeral broadcast on the radio in Sapulpa.

Both sanctuaries were filled with beautiful floral arrangements and both floral shops in Sapulpa were completely out of flowers. One spectator was overheard, saying: "There probably isn't a flower left in the state of Oklahoma."

Jerry Bailey's casket was placed in front of the pulpit and was already there as mourners filled the sanctuary. As people sat in the sanctuary pews waiting for the service to start, only hushed whispers could be heard, but most everyone sat in stunned silence. Only muffled coughs and sniffs from crying spectators could be heard. For over a day, the entire town wondered where Bailey could be, and now they wondered why he was lying in a casket only a few feet away. There were still no answers, and they weren't going to get answers anytime soon, but today wasn't about answers. It was about Jerry Bailey and the impact he had on several vastly different towns.

It was a crisp January day, and the high school administration asked the Bailey family if the funeral could be moved to the afternoon so teachers and students could attend. The funeral was originally scheduled for 10 a.m. but was changed to 2:30 p.m. to accommodate teachers, students and mourners driving in from out of town. The administration knew if the services were held in the morning the school would be empty the entire day. Again, the family obliged, and the time was changed.

Students were released from class at 2 p.m. to give them time to attend the services. However, the halls and classrooms were unusually empty throughout the day. Some students didn't report for school that day, and it wasn't held against them. Current and former players, as well as teachers, students and people who were forever changed by Bailey filled the pews to pay their respects to the coach. Loved ones from Sapulpa, Nowata and Broken Bow came to celebrate the life of their fallen friend.

Reverend Cook presided over the services and during an impassioned sermon he said: "The sum total of the life of Jerry Bailey measures up to a victory, not a loss. The race for Jerry was not near long enough in our estimation, but we have nothing to do with the length of life."

The entire Sapulpa football team was named honorary pallbearers.

People also spoke of Bailey's kindness. When describing Bailey, the title "coach" was too narrow. He was much more than that. He was also their friend. He didn't concern himself with only wins and losses; he was also concerned with the player's personal lives and how their home life was going.

On any given day he could be seen shuttling players back and forth from practice or school due to the harsh weather in Oklahoma. Every Oklahoman knows it's extremely hot in the summer and bitter cold in the winter. And if you don't like the weather in Oklahoma, stick around. It'll change.

Bailey didn't want his players walking several miles to get home after a lengthy practice, and he often filled the back of his El Camino with as many players as it could hold.

He also gave shoes and clothes to players that were in need. The coach cared about every player equally, but he also paid particular attention to the black players and how they were treated. They didn't get preferential treatment. He treated all of his players the same no matter their color, athletic ability or grade.

As far as race was concerned in Sapulpa, not much had changed since segregation. It reminded him of the restaurant his parents owned in Broken Bow and how the black players weren't always welcome when they came to town. However, the black players were welcome at his parent's restaurant, and they were welcome on his football team.

He would often drive to the predominantly black part of Sapulpa (also called "The Hill") and pick up several players so they wouldn't have to walk to practice. He would also take them home. His generosity towards the black players caused problems for some of the more closed-minded people in the community, but he didn't care.

Those were his players, and he was their coach. He wasn't a radical. He was human. He cared.

Bailey was buried in Green Hill Cemetery, and his funeral was under the direction of Owen Funeral Home. When Rev. Cook arrived at the Green Hill Memorial Gardens Cemetery, the parking lot was starting to fill up, and he could see a line of cars down Main Street. He was standing next to an officer when he heard a call over radio say there were still cars leaving the parking lot at the First Baptist Church. Traffic was backed up from the cemetery to the church and the two were about two miles apart.

Everyone that attended the funeral also went to the cemetery. The cemetery was packed, and even though most of the people couldn't hear Rev. Cook speak, they were there to pay their respects until Bailey was put into the ground. Beverly, Guy and Diedra received hugs too numerous to count, and a long line of mourners walked between the grave and the family to show they cared.

Students and faculty of Sapulpa High School formed a committee to determine how to best honor the memory of the late coach. The student-faculty group met with high school principal Charles Dodson on Sunday, the day before the funeral, to discuss the possibilities of establishing a lasting memorial.

Even though the Sapulpa Daily Herald newspaper had established an educational fund for the Bailey children, the committee wanted to do more. The result was the Jerry Bailey weight room and locker room. It became simply known as "The Bailey Building." The building was built through the tireless efforts of Bailey and his coaches, and the building wouldn't have been standing if not for their hard work and dedication. The building had been painted Chieftain Blue and was called the "Blue Building" before the name change.

When Bailey arrived at Sapulpa he knew the football team was outgrowing their facilities at Holmes Park, the football field and locker room at the time, and they had to acquire better facilities in order to compete with the ever-growing Tulsa schools. Bailey and his coaches spent countless hours raising the money and then worked off the clock to build the locker room. Today, the facility houses the high school football coach's offices, the high school football locker rooms and the junior high football locker rooms. There is also a state-of-the-art weight room.

CHAPTER EIGHT
Bailey's Reign at Sapulpa

The Chieftains started the 1971 season with a totally new look. The team had donned all-blue uniforms for the past several years, but the new season would bring blue jerseys, white pants, silver helmets and white cleats. Sapulpa needed a fresh start, and they got it with head coach Jerry Bailey.

The silver helmets were a staple of the Chieftain football program for years. Now, schools change uniforms every year, and some of the larger schools have five or six different sets of uniforms, and they can mix and match all season.

In 1971, the team's offense would look different as well. Bailey installed his diverse offense that included multiple formations out of the I-formation, pro-set and straight-T, compared to the option-offense that had been used at Sapulpa for years. Also, the team would throw the ball a whole lot more than they had in the past. Teams couldn't rely solely on their running game anymore. Football was becoming more complex, and teams all over the country were throwing the ball with success.

In the 1970s, the wishbone was king in Oklahoma, which meant running the ball. Bailey had to convince his team, the school and the community that his offense would work. They didn't need to look back any further than his last season at Nowata only a year before.

The 1971 Chieftain squad had several attributes that could mean a successful season, but they lacked experience. The Chieftains had speed, talent, power and ability, but the starters hadn't spent a lot of time on the field in game situations. Every season, graduation expelled most of the players with experience, and in 1971, due to the graduating class the year before, the Sapulpa backfield was thin, but the new players were more than capable of filling the shoes left by the former squad. There were some veterans.

Fullbacks Randy Reynolds and Jerry Morris were tabbed the starters for the Chieftains, and David Simmons returned as Sapulpa's main signal caller. Simmons was a smart, capable quarterback, and Bailey needed that type of player running his offense.

Sapulpa's offense consisted of smash-mouth power-running, and a short, accurate passing game. Reynolds, a 190-pound senior fullback, was described as a powerful runner that had good speed and the ability to wait on and follow his blockers. Sam Naifeh was the Chieftain's starting tailback and had good moves and quickness that provided a breakaway threat. Shan Moore and Jim Blankenship shared the halfback spot, and both had speed as well.

David Campbell, Randy Taylor, Richard Allman, Gal Gensicke, Bob Smith and George Smith made up the offensive line. The line was a bit under-sized, but had a lot of heart and the strength to open up holes for the backs to run through. Robert Titsworth, Curt Wilson, Marshall Cantrell and Davis Gray lined up at the receiver spots.

However, the biggest concern going into the season was the defense.

Despite a hefty defensive line with the Smiths, David Campbell, Randy Kelly, Dennis Hogan and Ronnie Moody, the linebackers were a problem area.

Linebackers Morris, Gray, Reynolds, David Edmondson and Eddie Ausmus had trouble defending the pass, but were very strong against the run. These boys had spent their entire lives defending run. That's usually all they ever saw.

The secondary consisted of Mike Osborn, Richard Davis, Moore, Mark Fox and Donald Lee, and all were considered above average. Bailey's first year at Sapulpa was his initiation into Class 4A football. Sapulpa would face power-house Okmulgee, Tulsa Bishop Kelley, Stillwater, Tahlequah and Tulsa Webster.

In the first game of the 1971 season, Sapulpa faced the Broken Arrow Tigers, a team they had beaten 9-0 in the season-opener a year before, but the Chieftains wouldn't be at full strength for its season-opener.

The team was dealt a bit of bad news the day before their game with the Tigers. Reynolds split his toe open helping a friend deliver newspapers for the Sapulpa Daily Herald and was out for the game. Bailey replaced him in the backfield with Morris, but Morris didn't have the breakaway speed of Reynolds. However, in a game-time decision, Reynolds decided, with encouragement from Bailey, to play despite his nagging injury. Bailey had a way of encouraging his players to fight through the pain and dig down deep to find that extra effort. After Bailey's private inspirational address, Reynolds decided to play.

Even with Reynolds in the game, Bailey lost his opening game, 20-14, at Holmes Park in front of 4,200 fans. The Tigers blocked two Sapulpa punts that resulted in touchdowns, burying the Chieftains for an 0-1 start.

Reynolds scored the first touchdown of the season on a one-yard run, but Broken Arrow answered right back with a 15-yard blocked punt return for a touchdown. Simmons picked up a one-yard TD run of his own and Sapulpa held on to a 14-6 halftime lead. Broken Arrow then scored 14 points in the third quarter with a 10-yard run and a recovered blocked punt in the end zone for the last score of the game. If Sapulpa didn't have any special teams break downs they could have easily won the game.

Reynolds was the team's leading rusher with only 57 yards on nine carries and one touchdown. However, the loss didn't concern Bailey. The new coach dropped his season opener at Nowata the year before and it seemed to eventually work out for him with the Ironmen.

"I'm not a believer in omens," Bailey told the Sapulpa Herald newspaper. "I thought we did a real fine job defensively and we showed the people that we are capable of playing football. The blocked punts were unfortunate. We knew we were weak in this area."

Bailey's first win came at the expense of arch-rival Sand Springs on Sept. 20, 1971 in a 13-10 Chieftain win. Every coach knows that as long as your beat your rival, you can keep the house and car for at least another month. After a 7-6 win over Pryor, Bailey had his first winning record as a Chieftain at 2-1, but it would be short lived.

The Chieftains then dropped five-straight games to Cushing, Tulsa Webster, Oklahoma City Northeast, Okmulgee and Tahlequah for a 2-6 record with only three games left in the season. Sapulpa then squeaked by Tulsa Bishop Kelley, 7-6, in the ninth game of the season, but fell to Stillwater and then Miami to cap a 3-8 year — not exactly what Bailey had in mind for his first year at his new school.

The 1972 campaign would mirror the 1971 season. With the exception of one less game played, Sapulpa followed with roughly the same win-loss record of 3-7. The Chieftains opened with a 44-6 loss to Claremore, but again, defeated arch-rival Sand Springs, 7-6. The Sapulpa team then beat Pryor for the second consecutive year with a score of, 7-6, for a 2-1 record. Sapulpa then lost five-straight games until another win over Bishop Kelley, and then a 36-14 loss to Owasso in the season final for the 3-7 season record.

The Sapulpa head coach would finally have success in his third season, posting the team's best record in several years.

The 1973 Chieftains jumped out to a 3-0 record with a 14-6 season-opening win over Claremore and another victory over Sand Springs, 21-14. The undefeated team then beat Pryor, 38-14, to stay perfect at 3-0 until a 37-0 rout by the Stillwater Pioneers. After another defeat from Tulsa Webster and a 6-6 tie with Okmulgee, Sapulpa had a 3-2-1 record after six games. The Chieftains then rattled off three-straight wins over Cascia Hall (26-0), Broken Arrow (21-14) and Bishop Kelley (37-0), but ended the season with a scoreless tie for the 6-2-2 record.

In five years, Bailey went 4-1 over the Sand Springs Sandites — the one team Sapulpa has circled on the calendar every season. The two towns are nearly identical, and that's why they don't like each other very much. They are separated by the Arkansas River and are only 10 miles away from each other down Highway 97. Each year, the game is played on pure emotion. Some games are blowouts and others are narrow one-point victories. On several occasions, the benches have cleared, and the players attempted to solve things with their fists or helmets used as weapons.

Both towns have a population of around 20,000 people with blue-collar families that support athletics while stressing faith above everything else. Depending on what side of the river you live on, the other side is always the wrong side.
*****

In 1974, the Chieftains were given a lot of respect by the local media due to Bailey's reputation and several key returning starters. Picked pre-season No. 1 by the Tulsa Tribune, the team got bit by the injury bug and ended the season with a 2-8 record. Several key players were lost for the season due to blown-out knees, a broken leg and suspension. This would be the only season that Bailey would lose to Sand Springs, and it was only by a 17-7 margin.

In his fifth season at Sapulpa, Bailey started the 1975 campaign with a 3-0 record like he did in 1973, but the team would wear out down the stretch, ending the season with a 4-6 record, going 1-6 in their final seven games.

Motivation wasn't lost on the struggling head coach, and he always had a few tricks up his sleeve. In his last season, his team was 4-4 and needed an edge. Sapulpa was playing the No. 1-ranked Bishop Kelley Comets, a Catholic private school in Tulsa, and Bailey wrote fake Halloween cards to several of his players, signing the cards "from the Kelley Football Team." They were hand-written with disparaging remarks regarding the Chieftain football team, the town of Sapulpa, and maybe even their mommas. Before the game that day, Bailey's coaching staff carefully placed the cards into the lockers and sat back to watch their handy work unfold. The coaches could hear the players yelling and screaming, full of anger and emotion. They had to defend their honor, the town, and the women who gave birth to them. The closer it got to game time, the more worked up the football players seemed to get at the top-ranked Comets. The team was seething just before kickoff, but the Halloween trick, played by the Sapulpa coaching staff, didn't work and Kelley treated the Chieftains to a 34-6 loss.

Several players eventually found out that Bailey had written the notes, and others still don't know to this day. Well, until now.

On the last game of the season at Holmes Park, the Chieftains lost 10-7 to Owasso on a last-second field goal that would have been the difference in a 5-5 season and a 4-6 season. Even though 5-5 isn't a winning season, it isn't a losing one, and it could possibly get a team into the play-offs. A 4-6 season might mean a playoff berth if the four wins are district wins, but Sapulpa didn't have enough wins in district play, and they ended the season with a 4-6 record.

After the loss, Bailey and his team walked through the stone entrance of Holmes Park to go back to the locker rooms located at the school a block away. Sapulpa boys basketball head coach Ray Reins put his arm on Bailey's shoulder and said, "Good game coach."

Bailey didn't answer, just smiled and nodded his head. He made the walk back to the school, and it was probably the longest walk of his life. Most Chieftain fans wondered if the head coach wanted to continue his run at Sapulpa, but his mind was already made up. After four losing seasons, the coach was ready to move on and try another school. Sapulpa had been Bailey's longest coaching job, but he was ready to move on. On Monday, December 8, 1975, a little over a month after the Owasso loss, Bailey turned in his resignation to Superintendent Dr. John Martin. The school board agreed that a change was necessary and accepted the resignation.

Rumors began circulating that Bailey was going to be fired, but he resigned, ending any need for speculation or conversation. Some say that the resignation was forced, but it was time for Bailey to try something new. The school was appreciative of his contributions and wished him the best.

"The program is certainly stronger than it was five years ago, due to Jerry's good leadership," Superintendent Martin told the Sapulpa Daily Herald.

Bailey told the Herald, "I feel very proud of what I accomplished here, but we need a new face for 100-percent confidence in being able to get a winning program. I feel I've used myself up trying to field a winning team. I don't know if I'll stay teaching; I may try another coaching job."

While at Sapulpa, Bailey's generosity knew no bounds, and he was there for his former players even after his resignation.

Sapulpa offensive lineman Ric Barnes was an above average football player and aspired to play the sport at the next level. On Tuesday, January 20, 1976, two days before Bailey's death, Barnes walked into his coach's office and expressed how he wanted to play college football.

82

"Coach, I want to go someplace and play football," he said eagerly. "I don't care where or for who. I don't care if I walk on or get a scholarship. I just want to play."

Bailey sat back in his chair and put his arm behind his head. He waited for the chair to stop creaking and said with a smile, "Ric, if you walk-on somewhere, you can pick and choose wherever you want to go. You can find the place that best suits you, but I wouldn't worry about it. I've got you lined up."

Barnes jumped to his feet, shook his coach's hand and walked out the door without saying a word. His eyes were as big as saucers, and he couldn't stop smiling. As he passed the weight room he grabbed the biggest dumbbells he could find and started lifting with more fervor and intensity than ever before. In his excitement, Barnes forgot to ask the coach one thing. The excited 18-year old didn't ask where the coach had gotten him a scholarship. He didn't care. He was going to play college football. Barnes trusted his head coach and knew where ever it was; it would be a good fit for him. His coach believed in him enough to find a college that wanted him.

Two days later, his coach was dead and college football was the last thing on Barnes' mind. He eventually went on to play football in state at East Central University, but he always wondered where he could have played.

During the 1975 season, there were a lot of talented players, and there was some jealousy about who was getting recruited and what colleges were being contacted. Bailey and his staff kept most of the college information confidential because it would have only complicated things. College recruiting isn't just about talent. It's also about attitude, grades, dedication and football IQ. When Barnes was long out of college, he ran into an old assistant coach from Sapulpa. As they talked about old times, Barnes found out that Bailey had got him a scholarship to play Division-I football at Texas Christian University.

*****

Race relations were important to Bailey. Every year the coach had summer camp at the high school and the players watched film together, practiced together and ate lunch in the high school cafeteria together. On the first day, the black players sat on one side of the lunch room and the white players sat on the other. Bailey walked into the room and immediately addressed the situation, telling the players to sit together despite their color. They were going to live as a team and a family.

Sapulpa was a predominately white, blue-collar, rural, hard-working community and that sometimes clashed with the new found freedom of the black community that lived on The Hill at the edge of town.

The head coach could be seen on The Hill with the black players, shooting hoops or giving rides to the ones that had to walk the four miles from The Hill to the high school. It caused waves in the early 1970s, but Bailey didn't care. He didn't see color. He saw young men who needed help and went out of his way to provide that help. It was also said that a compliment from Bailey went a long way and that he was the type of person that a player wanted to please.

After the Bristow Wrestling Tournament, the week he decided to step down as coach, several Sapulpa coaches met at the Woodland Lounge Bar, in Tulsa to relax. Bailey announced to Steve Shibley, Jim Stockard, Jerry Dean and a few others, that he was going to resign and take another head coaching job. The coaches tried to talk him out of it, but Bailey had made up his mind.

"I just can't get these guys over the hump," Bailey said sadly. "I'm very frustrated and maybe we just need a fresh start."

Bailey was looking at Sand springs, Enid and his home town of Broken Bow. When Bailey resigned, he asked his friend Jerry Dean if he wanted the head coaching job, and if he did, Bailey would recommend him.

Dean said, "I wouldn't take this job for nothing."

Bailey then told Dean that he had recommended all of his assistants and said that any one of them were ready for the job. Reagor and assistant Jim Stockard were the only assistants that applied for the head coaching position. Stockard was walking down the hall in the junior high about a week after Bailey's resignation when he was approached by Principal Charles Dodson.

"Let's go," Dodson said.

"Go where?" Stockard said.

"You're going to go apply for the head coaching job."

Stockard thought to himself, "I never came back to Sapulpa to take over the football program. I don't really want it."

Stockard was a legend at Sapulpa as a player. In the 1950s he broke the school's single-season rushing record and was considered one of the best running backs of all time in school history. He wasn't really prepared for the interview and by the time it was over, he knew he wasn't the right man for the job. He didn't answer a single question the way the school board wanted him to, and wasn't going to be a "yes man."

Dodson then asked Stockard if he still talked to Art Davis in California.

"Yes, I get a Christmas card from him every year," Stockard said.

"Do you think he'd be interested in the job?"

"Let's call him," Stockard said.

"Shut the door," Dodson said.

It was obvious to Stockard that this was going to be a secret phone call and that Dodson didn't want anyone to know what they were doing. The two called Davis and talked about the job. Davis said he was coming back to Sapulpa for the holidays and would contact them at that time. Davis came into town and immediately got in touch with Stockard.

Stockard told him he needed to demand the athletic director's job as well as the head football coach. Davis agreed and was promised the athletic director's position when Antwine Pryor resigned. He took the football job but never got to be athletic director. Bobby Lyons was hired as the A.D. when Pryor resigned.

Empty promises and misinformation was nothing new at Sapulpa.

On Friday, December 26, 1975, Art Davis, who had Sapulpa ties, was named Bailey's successor. The decision is believed, by some, to have sealed Bailey's eventual fate.

Davis, a Broken Arrow native, was an assistant coach at Sapulpa from 1957 to 1958 under Chuck Boyles and helped the team to an 8-1-1 record and an Oklahoma Six Conference Championship in his first year. Dodson lured Davis from Barstow High School in California, a school where Dodson had worked as an assistant principal while Davis was there. Davis played his college ball at the University of Tulsa and was a co-captain in 1956 and 1957.

Bailey personally recommended Reagor and Stockard for the head coaching job, but the administration chose to go a different direction.

CHAPTER NINE
Murder Charges

The same day Bailey was laid to rest, Paul Reagor Jr. was charged with the murder of his former boss. He was officially charged with second-degree murder in the knife-slaying of Bailey. Investigators made it clear that were no other suspects, and they were pursuing the theory that Reagor was convinced that Bailey stood in the way of his advancement at Sapulpa High School. After all, he did confess to the murder on several occasions to several different officers.

Reagor wasn't charged with first-degree murder because under a new Oklahoma statute at the time, first-degree murder only pertained to slayings committed during the commission of another felony, or other certain categories like government officials, police, judges etc.

Murder was the only crime for which Reagor was accused. He did not kidnap Bailey. The two were seen leaving the school together, and Bailey got into the car willingly and he didn't seem to be distressed when the two coaches passed Steve Shibley that morning. Reagor did not rob Bailey, the two were friends, and Bailey would have given him anything he needed. None of Bailey's property was found on Reagor.

That statute is no longer valid, and under today's laws, the crime would have fit a first degree murder charge. There was pre-meditation in the fact that Reagor stashed the knife in his car several days before the murder, and he planned on luring Bailey away from school to a secluded, wooded area.

On January 28, 1976, six days after the murder, Reagor was arraigned in the Tulsa County Court House and appeared on a stretcher. He was wearing hospital clothing and had a white sheet that was tucked in just under his chin. There were nylon restraints that looked like seat belts, tightly strapped across his chest and feet, securing his upper and lower body. Reagor was a patient, but he was also a suspect and had to be restrained for his safety and others. He was accused of murder and had tried to kill himself a month earlier.

Reagor refused to speak to the judge. He wouldn't enter a plea on his own, and a plea of "not guilty" was entered by the court. He was then ordered to be committed to Central State Griffin Memorial Hospital in Norman, Okla. for an observation period of no longer than 60 days.

Reagor was admitted for exactly 60 days and in that time period was treated by Loraine Schmidt M.D., Chief of Forensic Psychiatry. On March 24, 1976, Dr. Schmidt wrote a letter to Judge Ronald Ricketts, who was overseeing the case at that time.

The Honorable Judge Ronald N. Ricketts
Associate District Judge
Tulsa County
Tulsa, Oklahoma

Dear Judge Ricketts:
We have completed our psychiatric evaluation of Mr. Paul Reagor Jr., who was admitted to this hospital on 1-28-76 by District Court order for a period of observation not the exceed 60 days. The charges are: "Murder Second Degree."

We find that Mr. Reagor is mentally competent according to the laws of the State of Oklahoma. He is able to distinguish right and wrong and is capable of advising his attorney in his own defense.

As our evaluation has been completed, Mr. Reagor is ready to be returned to Court for your disposition. We would appreciate your sending for him the day you receive this letter.

Sincerely,

Loraine Schmidt, M.D.
Chief
Department of Forensic Psychiatry

This was the first time that Reagor was declared sane by a psychiatrist, and it wouldn't be the last.

Reagor was sent back to the Tulsa County Jail and started to exhibit the same psychological symptoms as before. He wouldn't communicate with jailers, refused to eat and just stared off into space.

On April 3, 1976, Dr. Norfleet again tried to interview Reagor in his cell, at the request of his attorney Don Gasaway. Dr. Norfleet had not seen Reagor as a patient since just after the murder.

On April 7, 1976, Dr. Norfleet wrote Gasaway a letter about his experience with Reagor. It read: *"I was allowed to enter the maximal security area at the Tulsa County Jail without difficulty. The jailer extended every courtesy to me, and I was escorted to the small cell occupied by Mr. Reagor. This is a windowless room. There are no chairs present, and the cell is illuminated by a small light bulb in the ceiling. I do not know whether Mr. Reagor receives a blanket to lay on at night or not. Nevertheless, there was no evidence of anything to aid the comfort of this unfortunate man.*

"As I entered the cell Mr. Reagor showed not the slightest indication of recognition. I remained in the cell with him for approximately twenty minutes, and at no time did Mr. Reagor respond to verbal stimuli. He was observed to have a very listless, apathetic expression. He appears to be extremely lethargic, and he shuffles around the cell more or less dragging each leg. I inquired about his family, and I also inquired about the treatment he had received at Central State Hospital from where he has been recently returned. He did not respond to any of my questions. Food was brought to him while I was interviewing him, but he

indicated no desire to eat any food. I specifically asked the jailer if Mr. Reagor was eating, and he informed me that he had eaten only very little for the past two or three days prior to being seen by the under-signed. It is my feeling that Mr. Reagor shows some clinical evidence of dehydration. It is my opinion that he should have some laboratory work done to see whether or not he is indeed dehydrated. It is my further feeling that if this is brought to the attention of Dr. Lyons something will be done to get the necessary laboratory work for this patient.

"Mr. Reagor did present a disheveled and unkempt appearance. He appeared extremely evasive and suspicious. He obviously was defensive during my interview. He showed no evidence of that he was able to concentrate. He was noted to be somewhat restless and repetitive. He actually does appear to be retarded. He made no effort to speak during the time that I was in his presence. No information at all was obtained about this patient. He does appear to be somewhat preoccupied with physical complaints. His mood is one of depression, but there is an overlay of rather moderately severe anxiety as well. His affect is flattened or superficial. It is difficult or almost impossible to do a real mental status evaluation on this patient.

"It appears that this patient is degenerating both emotionally and physically. It is my opinion that he has lost a considerable amount of weight since he was sent to Central State Hospital for further observation. It is my opinion that he is suffering with a psychosis and that the exact type of psychosis cannot be determined at this point. It is my feeling that the ultimate prognosis in regard to this patient is not very good.

"In my opinion Mr. Reagor is not competent at this point. I assuredly do not feel that he is competent to stand trial. He obviously needs some rather rapid definitive care if he is to avoid further mental and physical deterioration.

It is my recommendation that he be recommitted to the state hospital in either Vinita or Norman.

"I trust that this is the desired information. If further more specific information is needed it is requested that you inform the undersigned.

Sincerely yours,
Edward K. Norfleet, M.D.

On April 12, 1976, Reagor was then committed to Eastern State Hospital in Vinita for further evaluation. The defendant was evaluated for a two-week period and was found to have a treatable mental condition. Dr. Garcia requested that Reagor be committed to treat his mental condition so that he could be returned to court to stand trial.

Eastern State Hospital Superintendent Dr. Joe E. Tyler sent a letter to Judge Margaret Lamm, who was now presiding over the trial, advising her of the situation.

Superintendent Tyler wrote: "We have completed our coverage of Mr. Reagor, and it is the opinion of our staff that he is has a treatable mental illness which might interfere with his full cooperation with his attorneys. It is the recommendation of the staff that he be sent back to this hospital for a period of treatment, which should not exceed 4-6 weeks, and he should be well enough at that time to return to court to face the charges currently pending.

"We do not feel that a further period of observation is necessary, and we would recommend that he be returned to the court for further disposition. Please remove him from this hospital at your earliest convenience."

Reagor was then committed on May 6, 1976 for treatment of his "treatable mental illness." The patient was committed until June 10, and during that time, the doctors felt that Reagor was sane and in full control of his faculties.

In a letter to Judge Margaret Lamm, Dr. Garcia wrote:

"As a result of a recent evaluation it is the opinion of our staff that Mr. Reagor has improved to where he can now be considered sane according to the laws of the state of Oklahoma. He is able to accurately distinguish right and wrong and should be capable of advising legal counsel in his own defense. He is being maintained on the following medication: Triavil 4-25 q-i-d. (per oral), and we would recommend that he continue with this in order that his condition remain stabilized.

"Please remove him from this hospital at your earliest convenience."

On January 21, 1977, Reagor was again admitted to Eastern State Hospital for another evaluation and observation for a period of no longer than 60 days, per Judge Lamm.

Reagor spent a month in the hospital for evaluation and improved rapidly until he was ordered to return to court. He then had a relapse and was readmitted to the hospital.

During this observation, Dr. Garcia felt that the defendant was insane according to the laws of the state of Oklahoma. The psychiatrist said that Reagor was unable to determine right and wrong and would be unable of adequately assisting his legal counsel in the proper defense of his case.

He was then committed to Eastern State Hospital on February 25, 1977 for care and treatment and was released on April 22, 1977.

On four different occasions, Reagor was committed to the same hospital and found sane, and insane, by the exact same doctors. But this time, it would prove to be damaging to the defense and would be the "smoking gun" during the trial.

The day after he was readmitted, Reagor's symptoms miraculously disappeared.

After spending two months in the hospital, Reagor made an enormous breakthrough and began improving rapidly. However, when it would come time to leave the hospital and face the charges against him, Reagor would hyperventilate and become uncooperative. The defendant was malingering. He was not insane.

Staff Physician Dr. V. Vadhawker was one of the doctors treating Reagor and noticed all of the signs of someone that didn't want to go back to court and face the charges against him. He also noticed that when Reagor went back to jail, he would begin to show signs of insanity. But when he was under the care of a mental health facility where there were less rules and he was allowed more freedoms, the defendant would improve rapidly and would communicate and assist in his own treatments.

Dr. Vadhawker prepared Reagor's discharge summary, and it showed to be quite revealing.

ADMITTING DIAGNOSIS: Schizophrenia in remission.

FINAL DIAGNOSIS: Psychiatric: Schizophrenia, schizo-affective type.

Somatic: History of syphilis and prophylactic treatment with Tetracycline was given to him. His lumbar puncture could not be done, and it was not given to him. This time he did not show any signs of cardiovascular syphilis.

BRIEF HISTORY & ESSENTIAL PHYSICAL FINDINGS: Reagor, Paul is a 33 year old black married male from Tulsa County. He was the principal of a school in Sapulpa and had a B.S. degree in education. This was his fourth admission to ESH, and he was charged on January 4, 1977 with second degree murder. He was attending outpatient clinic in Tulsa regularly and was taking his medication. When his case came for hearing in the court he suddenly became psychotic, and the court had to send him back to ESH for treatment. First, he was on building 10 and then transferred to building 14 back on March, 3 1977.

COURSE IN HOSPITAL WITH COMPLICATIONS, IF ANY: The patient improved rapidly. He was cooperative and well behaved. In the beginning, he was not social but later became friendly. He used to play ping pong fairly well. While talking, he admitted that he was putting on all his psychotic symptoms. He was explained a few examples of court cases, and he agreed that it was of no use putting on and it was better to face the charges. His attorney had asked him to put on the psychotic act for at least three or four years, and he was under the impression that the charges would be dropped. He was explained that this would not be done, and he would have to face the charges after that period. He started behaving very well after that and said that he did not need any medication. His medication was discontinued, and he behaved very well with no problem. He was friendly, cooperative, well behaved and was socializing with everyone. He was re-staffed on April 7, and was decided to return him to the court.

CONDITION & PROGNOSIS ON DISCHARGE: The patient had improved satisfactorily, and he was very cooperative and well behaved. He did not show any psychosis and denied any hallucinations. He talked freely and socialized. He had no hallucinations or delusions and was on no medication. He was very eager to go back to court and face the charges. Prognosis is guarded.

EMPLOYMENT STATUS: No particular recommendations or restrictions for his employment. He was a coach and a teacher in the school and can go back to his job.

Dr. Tyler wrote a letter to Judge Lamm reiterating Dr. Vadhawker's diagnosis said that Reagor was completely sane and ready to stand trial.

Dr. Tyler wrote:

"During that period of observation the patient appeared to be functioning well until we were ready to return him to the court to stand trial. At this point he became mute, withdrawn, hyperventilated, and it became obvious that he would be unable to cooperate with his attorney in this trial. When the patient was readmitted to this hospital the day after his discharge from the period of observation, the previous mentioned behavior completely cleared up. During the past two months he has been in good contact with reality, has shown no histrionic behavior and is very pleasant and cooperative. He has received no anti-psychotic medication since February 8, 1977.

"Mr. Reagor is quite aware that he will never regain his freedom until he faces the charges that are pending and he claims he wants to return to court to clear up those charges. It is the opinion of the medical staff that Mr. Reagor is legally sane and can cooperate with his attorney if he chooses; however, we cannot be sure that he will not again become uncooperative as the time of his trial draws near."

From the day after the murder in January of 1976, Reagor was able to spend the majority of the time in mental institutions attempting to convince doctors of his insanity. He succeeded most of the time, but failed by April of 1977. There was no going back now. He was going to have to face a jury of his peers. He was going to have to explain why he killed his friend, Jerry Bailey.

Reagor's attempts to convince the court and the hospital of his insanity were thwarted and he was ordered to stand trial on July 9, 1977.

CHAPTER TEN
Sapulpa

In the state of Oklahoma, high school football is a way of life. To some, it's even a religion.

It's a religion that allows you to curse God and praise His name in the same breath. It's a religion that worships at the feet of coaches that can win the big game and condemns the ones that can't. It's a religion where more prayers can be heard in a stadium on a Friday night than in church on Easter Sunday morning. A religion where young boys, not even 17-years old, are labeled the next savior and are expected to revive their town by way of a state championship.

Make no doubt about it -- It is a religion.

The state of Oklahoma has only one professional sports team – the NBA's Oklahoma City Thunder. There are few minor league teams, but there aren't any NFL, Major League, NHL or Major League Soccer teams.

There is the AA Tulsa Drillers, an affiliate of the Los Angeles Dodgers and the Oklahoma City Dodgers, a AAA affiliate for the Los Angeles Dodgers, but there have been minor league basketball teams in the past, like the Tulsa Fast Breakers, and the Tulsa Zone, but none have ever made it past a few years. Arena football teams, the Tulsa Talons and OKC Redhawks, lasted only a few years. Most states have professional football, basketball, baseball and hockey, giving fans several sports to choose from.

Even though Oklahoma has an NBA team, the Oklahoma City Thunder, football is king and will remain king until the end of time.

For years, the University of Oklahoma football team was the closest thing to a professional team in the state. The Sooners are always a perennial favorite in college football and in the hunt for a national championship nearly every year.

With seven football national championships in the trophy case, more are sure to follow, and the team is treated with the same reverence and awe of any professional team in the nation. Former OU head coach Barry Switzer is referred to as "The King" after winning three national championships in 1974, 1975 and 1985. Bud Wilkinson brought Oklahoma football to the national stage in the 1950s with titles in 1950, 1955 and 1956, but Switzer brought the brash cockiness and swagger that remains to this day.

After a down period in the 1990s, head coach Bob Stoops revived the storied program and added another national championship in 2000 in only his second year in Norman, Oklahoma. He took OU back to the National Championship game in 2004, 2005 and 2008 but lost all three games. You have to be in championships to win championships, and Oklahoma has been there.

Saturday is designated for college football games, but Friday night is all about high school football.

The high school football season begins and ends in December. The Oklahoma high school state football championships are decided in December, and just days, sometimes hours later, coaches, players, parents, and fans try to figure out what went wrong, or how to win another one.

Some Oklahoma towns can boast of championship after championship, and others have never hoisted the gold ball. Some schools have sent numerous players to the collegiate level, and others have never left their home town.

In most Oklahoma towns, boys play for the same teams that their fathers played for 20 years earlier. The boys that grew up hearing about how their fathers won, or lost the big game, now make their own memories and write their own chapter in football's book of life.

Sapulpa subscribes to that religion and is a faithful follower.

The average-sized town is a suburb of Tulsa and is located only 15 miles away. The town is currently home to 20,000 people, and most have a long history there.

A full-blood lower Creek Indian named Chief Sapulpa was the city's first permanent settler. He was a member of the Kasihta Tribe in Osocheetown, Alabama and arrived in Indian Territory about 1850, establishing a trading post near the confluence of Polecat and Rock Creeks. In 1886, over 20 years after the civil war, the Pacific and Atlantic railroads expanded to the area, running past the trading post, and it was given the name "Sapulpa Station" in honor of Chief Sapulpa (he was never actually a Chief and was called that by white men out of disrespect).

In 1889, a post office named Sapulpa was opened, and the town was incorporated in 1898. Oil was then discovered in Glenpool, six miles southeast of Sapulpa, and the town grew by leaps and bounds due to the oil boom. The town exploded to about 20,000 people by the 1920s and housed four glass plants and two brick plants. Frankhoma Pottery, a company that made sculptures and dinnerware, was a big tourist attraction for travelers visiting the area for years. The pottery business started in 1933 and was located on Frankhoma Road, which is named after the company founder John Frank, who was a professor in ceramics at the University of Oklahoma.

Despite the success of the Sapulpa Lady Chieftains basketball team, who has state championships in 1979, 1980, 1998 and 2007, the town has always been a football town and always will be. The Chieftains are in Class 6A-II, which is the second largest class in Oklahoma after Class 6A split into two classes due to the larger schools winning everything. From 1995 to 2016, only Jenks or Union has won the state championship in football. Think about that. Only two schools out of around 30 have won the state title in football in over 20 years, and the Oklahoma Secondary Schools Athletic Association decided to split the class in two. Since then, only Bixby High School has won the Class 6A-II state football championship, earning a three-peat from 2014-2016. Only football was split. The other sports still have to fend for themselves against the much larger schools.

Broken Arrow, the largest school in the state, has 4,400 students enrolled, and they actually hold try-outs for the football squad. Tulsa Union has around 3,600 and can also turn away kids that aren't good enough for the team. Sapulpa has around 1,300 students enrolled, and everyone that comes out for the football team gets a helmet. Some students are given a helmet whether they want one or not. The Chieftains are a blue collar group of boys that have to work hard to be stronger and faster than their opponents. Most seasons, Sapulpa has one or two stars as opposed to Union or Jenks that have a roster full. Despite smaller numbers, the Sapulpa High School football program has had its share of winning teams throughout the years. The Chieftains have won district titles in 1978 and 1984 and can lay claim to conference championships in 1921, 1938, 1946, 1951 and 1955.

Sapulpa got their first taste of football in 1912 when the very first team was formed. The 11 players competed in only a few games, but in 1913 the school played its first full football season. They didn't really have a nickname yet, and Sapulpa wouldn't be the Chieftains for another 17 years.

The 1913 team had more wins than losses at 5-3 and played in an open lot near Park Street and Taft, right in the heart of town. In 1921, Sapulpa named itself state champions with a 12-1 record and was the first team ever to beat Tulsa Central. They did it in convincing fashion with a 33-0 route. They were the All-Southwestern Champions and claimed the state championship, but it isn't recognized by anyone else outside of Sapulpa, especially the OSSAA.

Nowata High School also had a 12-1 record the same year, and they claim the state championship, as well.

Three years later in 1924, Sapulpa was banished from the Athletic Association for dirty play and acquired the nickname the "Outlaws." The banishment lasted only a year through 1925, and three years after that in 1927, the Outlaws moved to Holmes Park at Hobson and Adams Streets. The new football complex was named after then superintendent Joe R. Holmes, and the high school games were played there for 49 years.

Two years later in 1929, Sapulpa changed its name from the Outlaws to the Chieftains, and the name has been controversial ever since. The year before in 1928, the school wanted to shake the negative "Outlaw" moniker and held a contest, asking students to suggest names for the team. A female student suggested Chieftains, and it was chosen for all sports. The Sapulpa Outlaws were now the Sapulpa Chieftains.

When girls sports teams were started for basketball, softball, track, swimming and cross country, they were called the Chieftainettes, but that was changed to Lady Chieftains in the mid-1990s.

Even though the word "Chieftain" is an Irish name for a leader, Indian groups in the area have protested the name and want it changed, claiming that it is racially insensitive. The school's mascot is a proud warrior, dressed in full headdress and war paint.

In 1929, Sapulpa played against the Tulsa Central Braves in the first-ever night game in the state of Oklahoma and, in 1938, the Chieftains were named co-champions of the Oklahoma Six Conference with an 8-3 record. The team earned the Oklahoma Six co-championship again in 1946 with a 9-1 season, but lost a playoff spot with coin toss.

Sapulpa celebrated its best season ever with the school's only undefeated season in 1951. Under the direction of Sapulpa coaching legend Bom Bomgardner, who is the school's winningest football coach of all time, the Chieftains posted a record of 10 wins and no losses, but they had one tie. Bomgarder's coaching career at Sapulpa lasted from 1943 to 1957, and in that span, the Chieftains posted a record of 78-49-10 to give the coach a 57-percent winning percentage.

In 1951, with two games left in the season, Sapulpa faced No. 1-ranked Muskogee, a team that was also undefeated at 7-0 and held a 4-0 conference record. The game would decide the Oklahoma Six Conference Champion and possibly the state champion.

Sapulpa was ranked No. 3 in the state and would have Muskogee on their home turf at Holmes Park in front of 7,000 screaming Chieftain fans. Both teams went scoreless in the first half, and the game would have to be decided in the last two quarters of play. In the third quarter, the Chieftains scored on a 5-yard run to go ahead, 6-0, but Muskogee half back Harry Tatum scored from 3-yards out to tie the game. The extra point attempt sailed wide, and the game ended deadlocked at 6-6. The Chieftains had to defeat Tulsa Central to at least share the conference title with Muskogee.

Sapulpa did just that, beating Central due to great special teams play by the kicker, who connected on all extra point attempts, which was the determining factor in the, 21-19, Sapulpa win.

Rumors spread that Sapulpa would play Muskogee in another game to decide the conference and state championship, but it never came to fruition and the two teams were named co-champions of the Oklahoma Six Conference, ending their seasons with 10-0-1 records.

The conference officials got together and decided that the schools wouldn't compete in the post season due to the fact it prolonged the season and infringed on the winter sports of basketball and wrestling. Most athletes were multi-sport athletes, playing in one or even two sports per season. It wasn't unheard of for some players to letter in football, wrestling, basketball, track and baseball.

"The state championship was postponed during World War II and then reinstated in about 1945, but the Oklahoma Six Conference decided to withdraw from the post season because of the winter sports, and they thought it extended the football season too long," said Charles Dodson, Sapulpa quarterback in 1951 and future high school principal and district superintendent.

In 1955, The Chieftains were 9-1 and co-champions of the Oklahoma Six for the fourth time in 18 years. The following year would be Bomgardner's last in a career that spanned 14 years at Sapulpa.

Nineteen seventy-six would see the first season played at George F. Collins Stadium on the campus of the high school. The team made the playoffs for the first time in the school's history in 1977 with a 5-6 record and was named district runner up.

The Chieftains would win the 4A-7 district championship in 1978, beating Tulsa Hale, 13-9, in the first round of the state playoffs. However, the team would lose in the state quarterfinals to Tulsa Memorial by one-point, 36-35. They won a second district title in 1984 with a 6-4 record, but lost to Tahlequah in the first round of state.

In 1989, Sapulpa romped Jenks, 33-13, in the first round of the state playoffs, making it their first playoff win since 1978 and the Chieftains wouldn't do it again for eight years.

In 1997, Sapulpa finished 8-4, took third in their district and beat Muskogee, 38-22, in the first round of the playoffs. However, they lost 42-12 to arch-rival Sand Springs in the state quarterfinals.

Despite several good football teams, the Chieftains have never advanced past the second round of the state playoffs. Sapulpa has also had some really bad seasons, including a 23-game losing streak that spanned four different seasons from 1979 to 1982. The Chieftains lost to Muskogee and Stillwater in 1979, went winless all 10 games in the 1980 and 1981 seasons, and then lost to Bristow in 1982 before beating Stillwater in the second game of the season.

The team has six no-win seasons in 96 years of football. In 1929, 1947, 1980, 1981, 2000 and 2008, Sapulpa couldn't manage to beat anyone.

Sapulpa is a town steeped in tradition. Every year, the Chieftains have a ceremony before the first home game called "The Burning of George." It started sometime in the 1950s or 1960s, but no one is quite sure when it started.

Most high schools around the country have an event that symbolizes the beginning of their football season. Some host barbecues or ice cream socials, others hold player auctions or watermelon feeds, but at Sapulpa the townsfolk prefer to hang a straw dummy from the gallows and burn him at the stake.

The ceremony is affectionately called "The Burning of George", where an effigy of the unknown George is torched. Many questions have arisen from these annual ceremonies that have gone unanswered for many years.

Who is George? What was his crime, and why do Sapulpans hate him so much?

George is usually burned at the stake, but he has also been tortured in years past. Due to burn-bans, Sapulpans didn't get to set him ablaze, so they found other ways to entertain themselves at his expense. George has been drowned, pelted with water balloons, hung, beaten with sticks, sprayed with a fire hose, and stomped on while the entire town watches with glee.

The burning is rumored to have started in the 1950s and at that time, Sapulpa played Stillwater High School for the first game of each season. Jim Harris, a coach at Stillwater from 1949 to 1969 doesn't remember a George at Stillwater, but did have a run-in with the Chieftains.

One year, the Chieftains typed letters and put them in the Stillwater locker room. "The letters said that they had spies in the school, and they had been watching our practices and writing the plays down, but we got to the fields late and didn't read the notes until after game. I think we beat them pretty bad," he said. Harris said he can't remember any George at Stillwater that was a player, principal or coach.

It is also rumored that George was a running back or a principal from Bristow in the 1950s. Rosemary Laforth is a native of Bristow and a 1941 graduate of the school and can't think of who it might be.

"I have gone to every game, and I can't think of anybody named George," she said.

Sapulpa began to play Bristow for their season opener in 1976 and the teams played until 1995. Sapulpa held an 11-9 edge during that time, and has a 25-16-2 series lead. The first time Sapulpa and Bristow met was in 1916, and they tied, 6-6. The last time the two teams played, Sapulpa won, 41-0, in 1995.

Former Sapulpa Superintendent Dr. Charles Dodson isn't sure about the origin of the burn either. Dodson played football at Sapulpa, and, professionally, has been a part of the school system in some capacity since the 1950s.

"I went to college in 1951 and came back to Sapulpa from 1957 to 1961. I left and then came back in 1971," he said. "When I came back in '71 (the burning) was already a tradition, so it must have started somewhere from 1961 to 1971."

Longtime resident and former town realtor Bob Nale said the event was going on as early as 1952 but wasn't around in 1949. Basically, the only thing that everyone agrees on is that they have no idea how or when the "Burning of George" started or who George is.

Whatever the case, George will go up in flames every year prior to the Chieftains' first home game, even though no one can say what he did to deserve such treatment.

CHAPTER ELEVEN
Race

The town of Sapulpa has been segregated since its inception, and, in some ways, still is to this day. The town is divided by a single hill. The black population lives on the hill just off of Line and Main streets located north of Sapulpa on Highway 97, heading towards Sand Springs. The area is still primarily a black neighborhood, and it's been called "The Hill" for a long time.

From the early 1900s to the 1960s, the black part of town flourished, was self-efficient and had several businesses, grocery stores, and its own school system. They had to. They weren't allowed to socialize, eat, learn or shop with the white community in downtown Sapulpa.

A black resident that lived on the hill didn't need to go to the white part of town, and they had all of the amenities that any other town needed: Booker T. Washington High School, Curry's Market, Jackson's Grocery, Joe's Barber Shop, G&W Cab Co., the Cozy Corner Restaurant, Lee's Hickory Barbeque, Dyer-Patterson Funeral Home and several other businesses. There was also the Oklahoma Baptist College that taught young, black women.

The all-black Booker T. Washington High School, named after the black educator from Virginia whose mother was a slave and his father white, was also located on the hill. They had their own sports teams and competed against other all-black high schools from the Tulsa area. They were not allowed to participate with other white high schools.

But that all changed on a spring night in 1960.

Texas, Oklahoma, Kansas, South Dakota, Iowa, Illinois, Missouri, New Mexico, Colorado, North Dakota, and Minnesota are located in what's called "Tornado Alley," a group of states where tornadoes are most frequent. Oklahoma is smack dab in the middle of tornado alley, and severe storms and tornado warnings are weekly occurrences in the spring time.

At 6:31 p.m. on Thursday, May 5, 1960 a tornado ripped through Sapulpa, damaging a large part of the black community. The tornado hit the hill, the tallest part of Sapulpa. For the most part, Sapulpa is in a valley and tornados usually pass by, but this time the town got hit. It got hit hard and without much warning.

The tornados that slashed through Oklahoma and Arkansas that evening killed 29 people and injured 250. Some of the area hospitals had to turn away the injured but tried to accommodate the seriously wounded patients.

Three Sapulpans, Lee Birmingham, Lillie Wright and George Thomas, were killed by the tornados, and 24 people were taken to Bartlett Memorial Hospital in downtown Sapulpa.

The 1960 tornado damaged the all-black high school building to the point that it couldn't be used or restored in a reasonable time period. The school year was almost over but there were a few weeks of class left, and the black students needed a school.

Sapulpa Public Schools had just built a brand new high school on Mission Street, and the school had only been in operation for less than a year. Since BTW was severely damaged, the Sapulpa school board was forced to make a decision. Superintendent Nole E. Vaughn and the board decided to move the black students to the high school and integrate them with the white students, but there was opposition to the school's decision.

The Civil Rights Act of 1964 eventually helped with the integration of white and black schools, but in Sapulpa, a tornado forced it.

Booker T. Washington High School opened its doors around 1910 in an old run-down wooden three-room building. In 1916, the school board decided that the small building was inadequate for future growth, and there needed to be a new building. A year later, a three-unit facility was built, and the new Booker T. Washington High School opened in September of 1917.

The school celebrated its first graduating class in 1923 with three graduates: Mary Harris and John and Tyree Galloway. The school flourished for 37 more years and offered numerous educational programs and vocational skills.

In 1960, black people in Sapulpa were not allowed to eat in restaurants, drink out of the same water fountains, use the same bathrooms or stay in the same hotels as whites. Some business and restaurant owners were sympathetic to their plight but couldn't show it for fear of retribution or loss of business. Some black people could be seen eating in the back rooms of restaurants or taking groceries out of the back of a store, but they could never eat or shop with white people.

This was six years after the United States government forced towns to integrate and allow black students to learn with white students. In 1954, the Supreme Court ruled on the landmark case *Brown v. Board of Education of Topeka, Kans.*, unanimously agreeing that segregation in public schools was unconstitutional. The decision overturned the 1896 *Plessy v. Ferguson* ruling that sanctioned "separate but equal" segregation of the races.

Before 1960, "separate but equal" was alive and well in Sapulpa with little opposition from either side. In 1955, in Alabama, Rosa Parks refused to give up her seat in the "colored-section" of the bus to a white passenger, leading to a boycott of the Montgomery Bus Transit. Two years later in 1957, nine black students attended Central High School in Little Rock, Ark. Until that point, the school had only taught white students.

In 1960, four black students from North Carolina Agricultural and Technical College begin a sit-in at a segregated Woolworth's lunch counter, sparking nonviolent protests across the country. Something was happening across the country.

At the time of the tornado in Sapulpa, there were no protests or sit-ins. The town was the way it was, but after the two schools integrated, the protests started, in a way, but not the way the protests were handled at the North Carolina Woolworth's or on a bus in Alabama. The protests at Sapulpa were held in the form of mistreatment, and it happened on both sides. It was subtle, but obvious at the same time, until the race riots in the 1970s.

Four years later, the Civil Rights Act of 1964 was enacted, "To enforce the constitutional right to vote, to confer jurisdiction upon the district courts of the United States to provide injunctive relief against discrimination in public accommodations, to authorize the Attorney General to institute suits to protect constitutional rights in public facilities and public education, to extend the Commission on Civil Rights, to prevent discrimination in federally assisted programs, to establish a Commission on Equal Employment Opportunity, and for other purposes."

Even though the Civil Rights Act was passed in 1964, the Sapulpa community had trouble accepting integration and there were race riots well into the 1970s.

Whether it was the fault of the white students or black students depends on who you ask. The riots were usually brutal, and several people got hurt, including the school's faculty. A group of white vocational agricultural students had a mean streak, tormenting the black students on a regular basis. A group of black students that were fed up with the treatment often went looking for fights, and they usually found them. When the two groups mixed, it was like throwing gasoline on a fire.

In 1971 when Bailey was offered the head coaching job at Sapulpa, he called his best friend Jerry Dean to ask him if he wanted to come and help him with the football team as an assistant coach.

Dean was at Wilson High School, in Wilson, Oklahoma, at the time but looked forward to coaching again with his long-time friend. While on the way to Sapulpa for the job interview, Dean and his wife were traveling down the Turner Turnpike near Bristow, listening to radio station AM740 KRMG when a Breaking News story flashed across the air waves.

"Stay away from Sapulpa!" the radio newsman said. "There is a race riot at the Sapulpa High School. Try to avoid the area. We will have more information as it becomes available. To repeat, stay away from the town of Sapulpa, especially the high school."

Dean leaned over to his wife and said, "Do you know where we are going, honey?"

Dean just laughed and kept on driving. His wife looked at him like he was kidding.

When they arrived, the parking lot was full of police cars, and there were people everywhere. During all of the commotion, He walked into the administration office and said, "I'm here to interview for a job." He was hired, and he got a first-hand view of what he was in for at his new job.

On one occasion, the white and black students squared off in the parking lot at the front entrance of the high school. The black students were in the parking lot and the white students were standing in front of the main doors to the school. Even though the black students had been attending school there for years, it was like the white students were daring them to enter the building. Something caused the rift, and it was probably insignificant.

The teachers and principals were standing between the two groups and seemed to have diffused the situation, until a soda pop bottle was thrown from the parking lot almost hitting the all-white group of students. The glass shattered at the feet of the white kids and all hell broke loose.

In 1974, Shibley was in his office getting ready for wrestling practice when he heard a commotion outside in the halls. By the time he walked up the stairs and into the main hallway, over 40 students, both black and white were fighting. It looked like a war zone.

Several of the faculty members were assaulted, and Principal Dodson received a cut over his eye. It's been said that black student, Fred Birch III, was the one who punched Dodson during the melee, but he was never charged or arrested. It was also just a rumor. The brawl was so chaotic, Dodson could have been struck by just about anyone. The incident was the last of the major riots, but they left a lasting impression on the town.

The building that housed the BTW High School was restored after the tornado and reopened as an elementary school until 1971. It then laid empty for three years until the city purchased it in 1974, and renovated it for the purpose of using it as a community center and the Booker T. Washington Recreation Center was dedicated on July 11, 1980.

CHAPTER TWELVE
Pre-trial

Assistant District Attorney Jerry E. Truster was given the task of prosecuting Reagor for the murder of Bailey and, for Creek County residents, only a conviction would do. Truster was a man of medium height and had a stocky build, but it was a muscular build. He was athletic and a big supporter of Ohio State University. In college, the Buckeye fan spent time on the sidelines with coaching great Woody Hayes, and, for Truster, the fall meant only one thing: Ohio State Football.

In Oklahoma, OSU football is big too, but the OSU stands for Oklahoma State University, located in Stillwater, Oklahoma around 60 miles away from Sapulpa. Truster's OSU was a few more miles away -- about 900 miles away.

Truster graduated from Ohio State with a Bachelor of Science Degree, majoring in psychology. He then went on to graduate from the University of Tulsa, College of Law, with a Juris Doctorate degree. He was hired as an assistant district attorney for Tulsa County in June of 1972 and was four years on the job when he received the Reagor case.

During that four year span, Truster was known as an attorney that would never back down. He viewed every case as a battle and saw each of them as a fight for justice for the victim and their families.

When Truster tried his cases, he could easily become adversarial with the defense attorneys, and when that happened, the gloves often came off. The prosecutor would spend countless hours reviewing testimony and case law, trying to find any edge that he could in order to debunk defense witness testimony to blow defense strategies out of the water.

Truster could prosecute with an iron-clad fist, getting witnesses to break through intense pressure, or he could use the "Colombo Method" and seem a little slow if he thought it might get a defense witness to slip up.

During a previous trial, Truster once asked a defense expert of Neurology if he was an expert in Urology to get a laugh out of the jury, and it worked. The joke relaxed the jury and made him an endearing figure. He won the case.

Truster became a student of trial law and had an unquenchable thirst for how juries worked, and the most effective way to present the facts of the case for the jury to understand. Truster also understood the importance of securing a conviction for the Bailey family. During the time leading up to the trial, he heard rumblings from the Sapulpa community.

"There was a concern from those in the Creek County area that we wouldn't put forth the same effort as if it were a Tulsa man that was killed," Truster said. "That just wasn't true. I felt very strongly towards the Bailey family and getting a conviction was priority one. Beverly, Guy and Deidre became very important to me, and I wanted to make this as easy as possible for the family so they could get on with their lives."

He would have to face the defense team of Don E. Gasaway and Barry Heaver, and it would not be the first time the attorneys had met in a high-profile case.

Truster was part of a team that made it a major priority to stop the sale of pornography in Oklahoma in the 1970s. The Tulsa County District Attorney's Office became very familiar with Gasaway and Heaver during the "Porn Wars," especially Gasaway.

Donald Eugene Gasaway was married and had two children. He had two passions in his life, other than his family -- the Law and officiating football. He attended the University of Tulsa and received degrees in Journalism and Law. Throughout his 28 year career of practicing as a defense lawyer, he argued successfully before the United States Supreme Court three times and served as the President of the First Amendment Lawyers Association.

His 50-year officiating career included refereeing high school, college, and professional football. He was one of a few chosen to work in the United States Football League (USFL) and the World Football League (WFL). Highlights of his career were working the Blue Bonnet Bowl and the Peach Bowl for college, and during the latter part of his life he worked the Arena Football League's first championship game.

But in the 1970s, Gasaway was busy defending people who had been arrested for violating Oklahoma's obscenity laws.

The arrests started around 1972, focusing on bookstores and movie theaters that sold magazines or showed movies that did not comply with obscenities laws in the state of Oklahoma.

They also focused on strip clubs. In Oklahoma, strip clubs in the 1970s, women could dance topless, exposing their breasts, but they could not dance without panties or bikini bottoms. In other words, they could dance topless but not bottomless.

In a September 1972 issue of the Tulsa World, a local strip club owner was arrested for breaking obscenity laws after a dancer was accused of dancing bottomless, exposing her pubic area. An undercover police officer was in the club when he noticed the dancer's lower half was exposed. While being questioned by the officer, the dancer emphatically claimed she was wearing a "fur bikini." The owner was arrested and convicted.

Gasaway was a very prominent, high profile attorney that represented pornography interests from out of state that would bring their product to Oklahoma, which is the buckle of the Bible belt. Pornography, tattoos and alcohol have all been taboo at one time or another in Oklahoma and pornography is still tame in Oklahoma compared to other states. Porn movies or magazines that are sold in Oklahoma are censored or watered-down. The images cannot show penetration or an erect penis. However, in the 1970s, certain parts of the female anatomy could not been shown at all. The female pubic area and pubic hair could be visible but the vagina could not. Hustler magazine founder, Larry Flynt began pushing boundaries in the early 1970s and was personally arrested for the pictures printed in his "Hustler" publications. Flynt was first prosecuted on obscenity charges in Cincinnati, Ohio in 1976. More arrests and charges followed.

Tulsa County District Attorney Buddy Fallis declared a war on pornography. Technology was moving at a fast pace in the 1970s but was still over 20 years away from the easily accessible internet, where one can get porn at the touch of a button. "Dirty book stores" were the outlet of choice back then, and some carried magazines with images that were illegal in Oklahoma. Some bookstores put them right on the shelves, daring the authorities to arrest them, and others would sell them out of the back of the store or from under the counter. Cash only, of course.

Fallis, and the rest of the district attorney's office, saw pornography as an off-shoot of the mafia and took these cases very seriously. The district attorney was not going to allow these slick, big-city mafia characters come in and soil the good people of Tulsa, Oklahoma. Gasaway and Heaver defended the principal players, including porn business owner, and old lady, Delta P. Wicks.

It's no secret that one of the most famous porn movies of all time "Deep Throat," released in 1972, was distributed by mafia-ran businesses, and the mob was heavily involved in porn. The movie also faced obscenity lawsuits, and some of the actors were tried and convicted.

Old Lady Wicks, as Truster called her, was "a little old lady that had a warehouse full of pornography and didn't look like a typical pornography distributor. She eventually had that warehouse full of porn raided by Tulsa Police, leading to the confiscation of boxes and boxes of illegal porn. Wicks was arrested and testified against her partners, securing at least 10 convictions for the Tulsa County District Attorney's Office, Truster said.

The police and district attorney's office combined forces to rid Oklahoma of this filth, and they even did their own dirty work.

In a case from August of 1972, Sergeant Frank Myers, Warren Henderson and Tulsa County Assistant District Attorney, Frank Hagedorn, appeared before a judge with books and movie film they had purchased from a local retail book store located in the Tulsa area. The charges were thrown out after a grand jury failed to bring charges, but an ex parte hearing was conducted, during which the judge viewed the material and determined the content to be obscene. Following the hearing, the magistrate issued a search and seizure warrant directing the officers to seize "magazines, photographs and multi-colored copies of materials showing acts of sexual intercourse and unnatural copulation between persons."

Pursuant to the search warrant, the Tulsa Book Mart, located at 620 South Main, Tulsa, was raided and all materials confiscated.

Two people were both charged with "trafficking in books showing acts of sexual intercourse and the sake of motion pictures showing acts of sexual intercourse." Gasaway represented the two defendants.

In 1973, Gasaway was involved in a case that involved a Presbyterian minister and college professor, a magazine that featured porn star Linda Lovelace and a junior college student.

The college student and part time store clerk was charged, tried and convicted in the District Court of Tulsa County for the sale of material containing photographs of "acts of sexual intercourse between persons."

Tulsa Police Officer R.E. Cartner said he entered the Sheridan Book Mart, an adult bookstore in Tulsa, for the purpose of serving an arrest warrant on an employee of the store. The clerk told the officer that the employee he was looking for had just completed his shift and was gone. The officer then browsed through the store and purchased a magazine entitled "Deep Throat." Before he bought the magazine, the officer asked the clerk if it was one of his "good books" and he said that it was. The officer also asked about Linda Lovelace and if she did "her thing" in the book. After the officer looked through the magazine, he arrested the clerk. The magazine, which contained explicit pictures of persons engaged in sexual intercourse.

During his trial, the defense called five witnesses, including the clerk. They also called Dr. Harold Eugene Hill, an ordained Presbyterian minister and associate professor of religion at the University of Tulsa. He testified that he used sexually explicit material during counseling sessions. Gasaway was attempting to have the materials deemed educational.

The clerk testified that he was a student at Tulsa Junior College and had worked at the bookstore for approximately two weeks. He also said that he had never looked through the magazine and that he had never made any statement to the officer concerning what was in the magazine.

The police and district attorney's office even asked for the public's help in winning the battle of the porn wars, using the print media.

In 1972, a store owner was charged, tried and convicted in the District Court of Tulsa County for the crime of the sale of a magazine showing acts of sexual intercourse.

During the trial, the state called one witness, Don Burris, who testified that as a private citizen he decided to help in response to a plea in a Tulsa newspaper. The district attorney asked for the citizens of Tulsa to help prosecute pornography dealers, and Burris bought the magazine "Heav-ly Bodies" on Sept. 9, 1972 at the Risque Book Store, an adult bookstore. The magazine contained explicit photographs of persons engaged in sexual intercourse. The Risqué Book Store lost several battles during the porn wars.

Gasaway also defended a man who was charged with selling "under the counter" magazines, literally.

In 1973, an adult book store clerk was convicted of selling a magazine which depicted "persons engaged in sexual intercourse and unnatural copulation." The original sentencing was a term of 15 years in the state penitentiary and a fine of $25,000.

Charles Sager testified that on Oct. 23, 1973, he entered the Whittier Book Store, an adult book store in Tulsa and told the clerk he wanted to purchase a magazine that "showed everything." The clerk reached under the counter, whipped out a magazine and stated that it was "the best he had."

Sager purchased the magazine titled "Erection" which contained pictures of people having sex. Sager also asked how he could get into the business and was told he could get some books at a premium price.

During the trial, the clerk admitted that he had sold the magazine to Sager. However, he denied having conversations about the book business and stated that he did not know exactly what was in the magazine. He also testified the only reason he told Sager the magazine was a "good book" was because it was high-priced and a sale would be good for the business.

The "Porn Wars" died down by 1976, and Truster was able to focus on convicting Reagor.

The Reagor trial wasn't an ordinary trial. Truster didn't have to prove that the defendant committed the crime, because he admitted it to three different law enforcement officers and several doctors. He also told them why and how he did it. Reagor did, however, plead "not guilty."

The assistant district attorney had to convince the jury that the defendant was sane at the time of the murder, and that he understood his Miranda Rights when they were given to him in the old abandoned farm house only 100 feet away from Bailey's body, in the ambulance, and at the hospital.

The prosecution had the confession, the body, and tons of evidence, but they didn't have a murder weapon. The knife used to kill Jerry Bailey was never found, despite a thorough search of the area by the farmhouse by several different law enforcement agencies. There was some confusion early in the search which might have led to never finding the knife. The initial report was that Bailey had been shot and then stabbed with a screw driver, but Reagor admitted there was only a kitchen knife, and that he threw it out the window of the car between the murder site and the farmhouse where the two coaches were found a day later. To this day, no murder weapon has ever been recovered.

CHAPTER THIRTEEN
Nowata

The town of Nowata was created in 1907 from Cherokee Lands in Oklahoma. The name is rumored to be a corruption of the Delaware Indian word "Noweeta" meaning "Welcome."

There are several rumors surrounding the name of the town, and one rumor is that two railroad surveyors asked an educated Delaware Indian woman what the town should be named, and she suggested the word "Noweta" meaning "welcome," which was then corrupted into Nowata.

Others say a Georgian, exploring the area, found several springs in the area to be dried up and posted a sign that said "No Wata" to warn other travelers.

Another rumor is that a drunken painter had misspelled "Noweeta," painting "Nowata" on the town's post office, and it just stuck.

Despite the peculiar name, there are plenty of springs and, contrary to popular belief, the town has running water. Ironically, in late 2016, there was a chemical plant explosion in Neodesha, Kansas, only 60 miles away, causing chemicals to get into Nowata's drinking water, forcing the town to first conserve and eventually go without water for a period of time. The town had finally lived up to its name.

In the late 1800s, there was actually a school in Nowata before there was even a town. Nowata's first subscription school was founded in 1890, and white children and Indians were taught together. The Indian children were allowed to attend the school for free, but the white children paid a tuition fee. There were 12 to 15 students in the one-room school, and Ida Mae Collins was the first-ever teacher. In 1903, the first graduating class of Nowata received their diplomas, and the ceremony had to be held in a large tent due to the size of the crowd. The complete accredited school system was organized in 1900, and a new high school was built in 1909 for $40,000.

The population of Nowata continued to grow and a new high school had to be built in 1918. A $315,000 bond was passed and the new school was built.

The town benefited from the oil boom at the turn of the century, and oil was found all over Nowata County. By 1905, there were oil pumps working around the clock. Several big oil companies like Sinclair, Phillips Petroleum and Forrest Oil got their start in the Nowata oil fields.

In 1904, Radium water was found when a drilling company was searching for oil, and Nowata became a hot spot for Radium baths. Known for its curative properties, Radium baths were all the rage and people traveled from all over the country to take a dip. The basement of the Savoy Hotel was one of the more popular "Radium houses" in town.

Uranium and natural gas were also found in town. Natural gas was plentiful and used almost immediately for commercial and residential use, but Uranium proved too costly.

With the oil and mineral boom came hotels, saloons and businesses.

The Williams Lumber Company, owned by G.E. Williams, was the first lumber yard in Nowata, starting just before 1900, and they were open until 1960. Lumber yards Farmer's Supply Company and John Knapp Lumber were also in business, and numerous hardware stores like the Nowata Hardware Store and the Simpson Brothers Hardware Store offered everything needed to build a house or business.

The Nowata Brick and Tile Company was one of the first industries to set up shop. The brick plant was only around until 1915, but some of the roads in town are made of brick, and Nowata Brick and Tile bricks can be seen on the foundations of homes that still stand.

There were more than a handful of hotels in town with The Savoy, the Carey Hotel, the East Side Hotel, The City Hotel, The Alluwe and the Hotel Campbell, just to name a few. Businesses were popping up all over town, like The Noxall Café, the Chuck Wagon Café, Ledington Cleaning Works, the Exchange Bakery, S.T. Hamm Barber, the Grand Pool Hall, Lambright Grocery, Wright's Notion Store and the Commercial Exchange Bank.

Cotton was a major commodity in the 1820s in Nowata County, but it was the Choctaw Nation at the time. Cotton crops were picked in the early fall and taken to local cotton gins to have the seeds removed, and then the truck loads were sent to Oklahoma City to be purchased by textile companies.

However, it was a major corporation in the 1980s that was the biggest boost and eventual decline in the town's economic growth. Walmart came to town in 1982, boasting of job opportunities and cheap prices on everyday items. It's both exciting and scary when big corporations come to small towns with big promises. Smaller mom and pop stores end up shutting down because they can't compete with the box store's low prices, and the customer becomes accustomed to the lower prices and convenience of the newer bigger stores.

Walmart was the town's biggest business and employed just over 70 residents, making it the No. 2 employer just behind the nursing home.

In 1995, Walmart closed its doors for good, opening a Supercenter in Bartlesville, around 20 miles away. The departure left a crater in the town's annual budget due to the loss of the sales tax, causing layoffs in municipal positions that weren't exactly non-essential.

Walmart wasn't just a place to get cheaper food, records and tapes, toiletries, auto parts, paint etc., it was also the social nerve center of the town. It wasn't uncommon to see ladies standing in the isles, swapping recipes or the latest rumor, or to see teenagers hanging out in the parking lot with their car doors open listening to the latest Def Leppard album or talking about Friday night's football game. Just like the numerous churches in town, Walmart had greeters, and those blue-smocked men and women could help you find the savings you were looking for.

When Walmart left town, a piece of Nowata's soul left with it.

But Nowata has one thing that can never be taken away from them, and that's football.

Football has been played in Nowata almost as long as it's been a town, and they were good right from the start.

In 1914, the Nowata Ironmen football team went undefeated with a 7-0 record and only allowed one touchdown. The team outscored their opponents 248-7 and is considered, by some, to be the best team in school history. It is definitely the best season statistically for Nowata, but again, there wasn't a state championship back then.

During the impressive 1914 season, the Ironmen defeated Collinsville, 26-0, in week 1, beat Chelsea 31-0 in week 2 and routed Dewey 43-0 in the third game of the season. They humiliated Wagoner, 54-0, in week 4, but gave up their only touchdown to Bartlesville in a 38-7 win in week 5. They knocked off Collinsville for the second time 27-0 and then ended the season with a 27-0 win over the Nowata Alumni.

Success breeds competition and interest. In 1915, the Ironmen had 24 players compared to the 11 that had played the year before, more than doubling players to choose from. In 1920, Nowata hired its first full-time coach, Lou Wilke, who was the coach for boys basketball, track and football. Nowata, like Sapulpa, also claims a state championship in 1921, but state championships weren't recognized until

1944, some 23 years later. It was also the year Nowata selected the "Ironmen" mascot for the football team.

Head coach Byrdene "Bom" Bomgardner coached at Nowata before he was hired away by Sapulpa and saw much success on the gridiron at both schools. Jerry Bailey also went from Nowata to Sapulpa, following in the footsteps of Bomgardner. At Nowata, Bomgardner ended with a 30-8-2 record, coaching there from 1939 to 1942. After his first season, he didn't lose another game until he resigned, going 28-0-2 in his last three seasons.

Bob Paige was a tailback at Nowata in the 1940s under Bomgardner, and he is related to Dee Paige, who quarterbacked the team in 1970.

"Bomgardner was a great coach," said Bob Paige. "He had three undefeated seasons at Nowata before he went to Sapulpa, and I think that he only had one tie in those three years.

"Under Bomgardner in the 1942 undefeated season, Nowata laid claim to another state championship and was the only team with two All-State players that year. He was also the basketball coach, and he coached both sports without any assistants."

That year, Lewis Ray Dunn and Bennie Ballard were named to the All-State team, but both were killed in World War II. Bomgardner was elected into the Oklahoma Coaches Hall of Fame in 1977.

The Ironmen have won district titles in every decade since 1940, winning district championships in 1945-46, '51, '53, '65, '70, '74, '83, '87-88, '99 and 2004, but the year people still talk about is the 1970 season.

In 1988, the Ironmen earned a spot in the 2A state title game against highly-touted Wynnewood, but lost, 35-7, in their first state championship appearance in 18 years.

Nine years later, a movie titled "Possums" was filmed in the town of Nowata, and the film's subject was football. The movie was about a small town that loses its spirit when the high school football season is canceled after 25 losing seasons. Mac Davis, star of the classic football movie "North Dallas 40," starred as a hardware store owner and volunteer sports announcer who begins broadcasting imaginary games about the team, dubbed the "Possums" because they would basically lie down and play dead for their opponents.

The state champion Prattville Pirates, a high school that doesn't actually exist, hears about the successful Possums and challenges the team to a game. Former Oklahoma Sooners head coach Barry Switzer makes an appearance as the Pirates' head coach, making an inspirational address to his team during the half time of the big game.

The Possums lost the game but scored their first touchdown in nearly 15 years. The movie was truly fiction, because Nowata is always a contender in Class 2A and has advanced to the state title game at least five times.

The actual Nowata team found its way back to the state championship again in 1999, but lost to Davis High School. The Ironmen had an undefeated record at 13-0 with the district title, but they couldn't get past Davis. In 2014, the Ironmen were back in the state championship again, and guess who was waiting for them? Davis High School.

Davis beat Nowata, 20-13, for an undefeated season and its sixth state football title, and Nowata ended the season 14-1.

The accomplishment was quite impressive. Only three years earlier, Nowata went through a dark period of football when most of the team quit before the season even started. Head coach Randy Zabel was hired to guide the Ironmen in 2011, but he was fired before coaching in a single game. The players refused to play for the new coach, quitting before a preseason scrimmage only weeks before the opening game. Zabel was fired, and an assistant coach led the team to an 0-10 season. Matt Hagebucsh was hired as the new head coach for 2012.

After being hired, Hagebusch told the Tulsa World, "They've been in the state championship game every decade since 1970," he said. "They're used to being in the playoffs, and not just being in it, but making deep runs in the playoffs."

If that was a promise to take the Ironmen back to the state playoffs and the state championship game, he lived up to that promise. Two years later, they were fishing for a state title. After the 2014 loss to Davis in the championship, Hagebusch resigned and took the head coaching job at Claremore Sequoyah. He was 40-10 at Nowata.

CHAPTER FOURTEEN
The 1970 Football Season

Expectations were high in Nowata in 1970. Just as high as any other year in the football crazy town, but after the first three games of the season, the town had all but given up on the Ironmen.

At the beginning of the year, both the Tulsa World and Tulsa Tribune newspapers picked the Ironmen to finish towards the middle or at the bottom of district 2A-6. The Tulsa World picked Nowata to finish fourth in the Verdigris Valley Conference after a 3-6-1 season the year before in1969, head coach Jerry Bailey's first year.

The 1970 season was considered a rebuilding year to some, but Nowata had several starters back, most importantly, senior quarterback Dee Paige. He was the team's main signal caller and was more than just a quarterback; he was also considered a coach on the field.

Paige called his own plays from the huddle, which was, and still is, unheard of at any level of football. Even NFL quarterbacks have headsets in their helmets, allowing coaches to call the plays in the huddle. Most football coaches are control-freaks and want to be in charge of the game, but Bailey had confidence in Paige's ability and turned the game over to him at kickoff.

The senior quarterback was confident, but not cocky. He was an introvert, very intelligent and depended on his brain as much as his athletic ability. Paige was not a big, dumb jock. He was a cerebral quarterback that was able to read the opposing defenses and would choose the plays according to the flow of the game.

He could throw the ball with ease but could also tuck the ball and run when flushed out of the pocket. He was a run-pass quarterback and was efficient at both.

Junior Rick Reid and senior Bruce Campbell were Paige's main receivers, and senior Tom Dennis was the team's work horse at tailback.

The offensive line consisted of center Chuck Miller, guards Larry Johnson and John Richardson and tackles Woody Teel and Mike Morris. Defensively, Ken Griffin, Danny Covey, Mike Jones and Justin Pugh tried to keep opposing offenses out of the Ironmen end zone.

There were only 30 student-athletes that came out for the team and they were affectionately called the "Dirty Thirty."

On Sept. 11, 1970, week 1 went very badly for the Dirty Thirty when No. 6-ranked Dewey beat them by 20 points, 32-12. The game was never in doubt, and Dewey rolled to a 1-0 start. Nowata was 0-1.

In week 2, the Ironmen tied Collinsville, 6-6, for the 0-1-1 season total, and on Sept. 26, Nowata was shut out by Pawhuska, 15-0. The newspapers looked as if they were right about their pre-season predictions, and maybe they were being too generous. The non-district games were now out of the way, but those were supposed to be the tune-up games before the real season started – district play. The next seven games would determine who goes to the playoffs. The Ironmen were in Dist. 2A-6, a very tough district.

The townsfolk and the students at the high school were starting to think the season was over, and as far as the rest of Class 2A was concerned, the Ironmen could have just forfeited the rest of their games and given up, but that's not Nowata.

The strain was also starting to show with some of the players. Dee Paige, the starting quarterback and leader of the team, was so upset with his play on the field he wanted Coach Bailey to play the back-up quarterback, Dutch Dunn. The senior signal caller put a lot of pressure on himself and didn't feel that he was making the right choices at his position. The depressed quarterback went to Bailey and asked the coach if he would bench him. He was actually trying to bench himself.

Bailey looked at Paige and said, "No, Dee. You're our quarterback and we're going to stick with you." The confidence Bailey had for Paige seemed to rub off on the struggling senior, but Paige needed to get out of his funk and get out of it quick. District play was starting, and those games were the only games that mattered.

Nowata faced Tulsa Union in week four, and they trounced the Redskins, 33-6, for the team's first win of the season. Before that game, the Ironmen had been outscored by their opponents 53-12 and, in one game, narrowed that statistic to 59-51.

On Oct. 10, the Ironmen continued to roll, beating Stillwell, 20-12. Nowata now had an even win-loss record at 2-2-1. Stillwell was picked to win the district, and the eight-point win seemed to turn the season around, but there was a lot of season left – five games, actually. Nowata had finally defeated a team that was supposed to beat them handily and confidence started to spread to the players and the community.

In week 6, Nowata pummeled Locust Grove 51-0 and recorded their first shut out of the season. At 3-2-1, Nowata now had a winning record, and everything seemed to start clicking for the Ironmen and the first three games of the season were just a distant memory.

In weeks 7 and 8, Nowata beat Jay 42-0 and Wagoner 27-15 for a five-game winning streak, and week 9 wouldn't be any different when Nowata beat Vinita, 32-6.

On the last game of the regular season, with a 6-2-1 record, Nowata found themselves playing for the Dist. 2A-6 championship, and the team was riding a six-game winning streak. After going winless in their first three games of the season, Nowata had now earned a playoff berth and, in just a few hours, could claim the district title. What do sports writers know anyway?

The Dirty Thirty had now earned their nickname, and the Catoosa Indians were standing in the way of a district title. It was time to get dirty, literally. The game was played at Catoosa High School, located just outside of Tulsa, and the football stadium was in a field out in the middle of nowhere. It was a bitterly cold night and it had rained all day. The field was a muddy mess with standing water.

The game clock kept moving because both teams ran the ball without much success and they stayed in bounds, allowing precious seconds to tick away. However, the players would feel like it was an eternity due to the harsh conditions. Their white uniforms were stained brown and each player was covered in the gooey mud, causing some of them to blend in with the ground after each play was over.

Nowata fullback Tom Dennis scored the game's lone touchdown on an 11-yard run, and Nowata beat Catoosa, 7-0, to claim the district trophy, advancing to the 2A state playoffs.

Nowata wasn't supposed to make any noise in the district, much less win it. But they did, and people were starting to take notice of this team. Well, people in Nowata were taking notice. Outside of the small town, the Ironmen still weren't receiving any respect.

The town was crazy with Ironmen fever. Downtown Nowata, which is a street about a half-mile long, was littered with Maroon and White. Hand-painted signs that read: "Where is Dewey?" and "All the Way Nowata" and "Take State" could be seen on store front windows, and everyone was talking about the "Dirty Thirty."

With a 7-2-1 record, the Ironmen had to face the Dewey Bulldogs again, but this wasn't a non-district game. It was the first round of the Class 2A playoffs.

Everyone thought Nowata's season was pretty much over; everyone outside of Nowata that is. After all, Dewey had beaten the Ironmen by 20 points in the first week of the season. Dewey was now ranked No. 4 in the state, and Nowata was sitting at No. 10.

However, these were two teams going in different directions. Dewey was back on its heels and still reeling from a 14-0 loss to the Claremore Zebras in their last regular season game. It was their first loss of the season, and the Bulldogs were ranked No. 2 until the loss to the Zebras.

Class 2A No. 4 Dewey (9-1) and No. 10-ranked Nowata (7-2-1) locked horns in an epic battle, and the Ironmen pulled off a dramatic win, 27-20, in what was called the state's biggest upset. Nowata had been unranked all season, but that didn't seem to matter now. Winning their last game of the season was all that mattered.

Everyone had written off the Ironmen, but the team was able to avenge the embarrassing loss from week one, proving nearly everyone wrong. The team had a lot of confidence after winning seven-straight games and Dewey seemed be too confident.

In the game, Dewey drew first blood and scored on a one-yard run for the 6-0 Bulldog lead, but Nowata quarterback Dee Paige answered right back with a one-yard run of his own, and the Ironmen took a 7-6 lead. Paige relied on his legs again, scoring on another one-yard run, and Nowata had the Bulldogs by the collar, 14-6.

Dewey scored its second touchdown in the third quarter and connected on the two-point conversion for the 14-14 tie. Paige then showed the crowd that he can also throw the ball when he hooked up with Rick Reid for a 26-yard touchdown pass.

With a 20-14 lead in fourth quarter, Nowata gave up a 36-yard touchdown run and the game was again tied, 20-20. Reid then took it upon himself to finish off the Bulldogs, scoring the game-winning touchdown on an 18-yard run. However, Reid didn't put Dewey away with his legs -- it was his hands that stopped the Bulldogs.

With 1:54 left in the game, the junior receiver/defensive back intercepted Dewey quarterback Steve Dittman on the

Nowata 25-yard line to seal the Bulldog's fate. Reid ended the game with four interceptions on defense and two touchdowns, offensively. He was clearly the game's MVP.

Bailey refused to pick out one particular player that shined in the game and named virtually everyone on the roster as "player of the game." He even credited the cheerleaders with helping the team by cheering loud and getting the crowd into the game.

Bailey did credit his defensive line, led by Mike Jones, Danny Covey, Justin Pugh and Ken Griffin. The front four of the Dirty Thirty held Dewey to under 100 yards rushing, and the season-opening, 32-12, loss to the Bulldogs meant nothing now.

The Ironmen even got the Tulsa Tribune newspaper to admit they were better than their No. 10 ranking. What do sports writers know anyway?

After the first-round playoff win, the team was celebrating in the Ironmen locker room until Coach Bailey decided to address the players. Everyone was waiting for the coach to tell the team how proud he was of them for doing the impossible.

Instead, Bailey looked at the team with a half-smile and said, "Now you guys have blown yourself out of a vacation." The locker room erupted with a deafening cheer, and the team knew they had just done something special, but it wasn't over. They had to win two more games, and all of the other teams in the playoffs were ranked ahead of them.

The headline of the Tulsa Tribune read: "Nowata Sends Dewey on Early Vacation."

However, there would be no vacation for Nowata, and the Ironmen had to work if they wanted to stay alive in the playoffs.

That same night, No. 1 Lindsay beat Wewoka, 26-6, Watonga beat Elk City, 17-14, and No. 2 Sallisaw hammered Madill, 47-7, to advance to the next round.

Nowata's win set up a semi-final match up against the No. 2-ranked Sallisaw Black Diamonds.

This had to be the end for Nowata.

There was no way the Ironmen could beat Sallisaw. The ride was fun, but it was over. It had to be. There is no way a team can pull off that many upsets in a row. Nowata definitely left everything they had on the field against Dewey, right?

Sallisaw had one of the best quarterbacks in the state in Steve Davis, a University of Oklahoma commit. Nowata had a bunch of no-name players that had gotten lucky the past couple of weeks. Sallisaw was 10-1, and Nowata had started the season 0-2-1. The Black Diamonds had been ranked in the top ten all season, and Nowata was unranked until the first round of the state playoffs.

Someone forgot to tell the "Dirty Thirty" all of these things because when the whistle blew on Nov. 28, rankings, records and high-profile players went out the window.

Sallisaw scored first and took a 6-0 lead in the first quarter, but Nowata running back Tom Dennis answered back with a 2-yard score, and the teams were deadlocked at 6-6 after the first quarter. Nowata was held scoreless in the second quarter and trailed 13-6 after a Steve Davis touchdown run from the 1-yard line. Nowata would go into the locker room trailing by seven points, but the Ironmen hadn't given up.

In the third quarter, it was Sallisaw's turn to go scoreless, and Rick Reid pulled his team within one point on a 42-yard TD run. Down 13-12 in the fourth quarter, Paige dropped back and hit Reid for a 69-yard Ironmen touchdown to win the game, 18-13.

Penalties killed Sallisaw, and Paige executed the offsides play to perfection, getting the defense to jump across the line of scrimmage before the snap. The Black Diamonds were too eager to get to Paige, so he changed his signal cadence to confuse them. It worked three times in a row.

Nowata's snap count always went on the count of one – down, set, hut! Paige changed the count to two, and the defense bit every single time – down, set, hut, hut!

Dropped passes also hurt Sallisaw on offense. The team's tight end got behind the Nowata defense all game, but several of Davis' passes that could have resulted in big plays were dropped.

Again, it was a major celebration in the Nowata locker room with players, coaches, trainers, teachers, the school administration, cheerleaders and parents. However, the celebration would be short lived. Shortly after the game, Nowata found out they would play top-ranked and undefeated Lindsay for the state championship.

The No. 1-ranked Lindsey Leopards easily beat Watonga, 22-8, in their semifinal game, and Nowata would have to face the top team in the state for the Class 2A state title. Again, it was a good run. It had to be the end.

The Lindsay Leopards didn't just beat teams; they punished them. In week one, Lindsay beat Purcell, 34-0, and Yukon was their next victim at, 30-0. Oklahoma City Crooked Oak would fall, 47-0, and Marlow lost to the Leopards, 36-0. Lindsay didn't give up its first touchdown defensively until week five. They won, 57-6. To this point, Lindsay had outscored their opponents 204-6. If this was the fictitious movie "Possums," Lindsay would be the Prattville Pirates, and Nowata would be, well, they'd still be Nowata.

Lindsay sailed through the season and the playoffs to end up in the state championship game. After all, they had been ranked No. 1 all year long and the title game was more of a formality. They had to play the game, but no one would have been surprised if the OSSAA started engraving Lindsay's name on the state trophy a week early.

On Thursday before the game, the Ironmen sat down to eat their team meal together. Senior defensive end Ken Griffin got a hold of the Edmond Sun newspaper that predicted a 35-point victory for Lindsay.

Griffin stood up and said with a loud voice, "Hey guys, the paper said were going to lose by 35 points." The room erupted with laughter, but the laughter soon turned into anger and the entire Ironmen football team was fired up. They had been disrespected all season long, even after beating teams that they weren't supposed to. No one respected Nowata, and now they had "bulletin board material" to stare at and think about for two days.

It was David versus Goliath.

The state championship game was played on Friday, Dec. 4, 1970 in Edmond's Wantland Stadium, home of the Central State College Bronchos. A year later, the school changed its name to Central State University, and now, it's the University of Central Oklahoma. The stadium was bigger than anything the Ironmen had ever played in. It was huge. It was shaped like a horseshoe. The home and away stands were connected by a sloped piece of land behind one of the end zones with the scoreboard above it. The other end zone was the open part of the horseshoe. The visiting side was also a sloped piece of land, and spectators could sit on the grass with blankets, but there were also concrete seats. The home stands had blue reserved seats in the middle with regular benches on each side.

Both end zones had the college's mascot "Bronchos" painted in yellow and blue, and the school's logo was on the 50-yard line.

Nowata had already been dubbed "Cinderella" by the local media, and the clock was about to strike midnight.

During warm-ups, Nowata quarterback Dee Paige walked out of the locker room and looked over at the players on the Lindsay side of the field. He stopped counting them and just guessed that there were around 80 players wearing a Leopard uniform -- 80 players to Nowata's 30, but they were the Dirty Thirty.

The game started just like everyone thought it would. Lindsay scored two touchdowns in one-minute and sixteen seconds, and Nowata was down, 12-0, very early in the first quarter. A fumble by Paige and a fumbled kick-off return allowed highly-touted Leopard running back Mike Terry to put points on the board, and Cinderella was about to turn back into the poor maiden, banished back into the cellar.

Terry, who went on to play defensive back at Oklahoma State University, scored on runs of 3 and 20 yards for the first two scores of the game.

On the next offensive series, Paige threw an interception to give Lindsay the ball with good field position. However, the No. 1-ranked team failed to score and still had a 12-point lead, but Bailey wasn't worried. His team had just turned the ball over on their first three offensive series, resulting in two scores, but Bailey was calm as could be given the situation.

The Nowata head coach told the Tulsa Tribune, "As soon as we lost the ball three times I knew we were ready to play. Seriously, I wasn't worried. I just thought, 'Here we go again.' I don't know what it is, but we don't start playing until we lose the ball a few times. It looks like we coach that stuff," he laughed.

Down 12-0 at halftime, Nowata was out rushed 113 yards to 44 and most of the yards were from Terry. It all turned around in the second half when Nowata's Justin Pugh recovered a fumble deep in Lindsay territory early in the third quarter.

Then, Paige went to work.

The senior quarterback began dissecting the Lindsay defense like a skilled surgeon. The drive culminated in a 9-yard touchdown pass from Paige to Bruce Campbell for Nowata's first score of the game. The Ironmen were on the board, and the momentum was changing.

136

What ended up being even bigger than the touchdown was Ivan Walker's extra point. The sophomore kicker was a straight-on place-kicker that used his toe, splitting the uprights for the 12-7 score. Nowata was down only five points, but Lindsey was still ranked No. 1 in the state, and it was just a matter of time before they started playing like it.

Paige and his team had something else in mind.

On the next series, after holding the Leopard offense, Paige threw another touchdown pass, this time to Rick Reid, his favorite target. The 40-yard score put the Ironmen ahead, 13-12, and just like that, Lindsay was scrambling to find an answer. The game turned, in a matter of two offensive series, and the crowd that was silenced in the first half was now in a frenzy, cheering louder than any Nowata crowd had ever cheered before.

Kicker Ivan Walker had already nailed his first extra point and he hit the other with the same poise. It was now, 14-12, Nowata.

The top-ranked and undefeated Lindsay Leopards were down, 14-12, to the barely-ranked Nowata Ironmen, but there was another quarter to play, and the Leopards were averaging 40 points a game.

In the fourth quarter, Nowata's defense took over, taking it upon themselves to give their town its first-ever football state championship recognized by the Oklahoma Secondary Schools Athletic Association.

The Ironmen held the Leopard offense and stopped them four times inside the Nowata 15-yard line, including a final stop with only five seconds left in the game.

As the game clock read 0:00, Cinderella, who was living in unfortunate circumstances, was now celebrating an unbelievable fortune. The glass slipper was transformed into a gold ball in the shape of a football, and the Ironmen lived happily ever after.

Down on the field, the players rushed the 50-yardline, crying and hugging each other, shedding tears of joy, but only five short years later, they would be crying and hugging each other again for a completely different reason.

By the end of the game, Lindsay led in every statistical category accept one – the score.

The difference in the game was two points, actually two extra points. Lindsay place-kicker Bud McGuire had connected on 35-straight point after attempts in the regular season, but missed two in the biggest game of the season.

While the Nowata team was in the locker room dancing, singing and celebrating, Paige secluded himself to a corner away from the noise and jubilation to reflect on what had just taken place.

"I can't believe it," he said in his head because he couldn't actually vocalize the words. "We just beat the best team in the state, and we were a 35-point underdog. I can't believe it."

The Dirty Thirty that started the season with two losses and one tie were now heroes in a fairy-tale story that would be told and retold for years to come.

David struck Goliath with his sling, and the mighty giant fell.

The Nowata Star Newspaper reported, "...The only thing that marred the happiness of the Nowata crowd was speculation on the size of salary some of the larger schools are probably mentioning in conversations with head coach Jerry Bailey."

After the season was over, the awards and accolades didn't help comfort the town's fears. Bailey was honored with the Verdigris Valley Coach of the year, the Tulsa World Coach of the Week and 2A Coach of the year awards. The mission was accomplished, and it was time for the head coach to move on.

On Feb. 1, 1971, Bailey tendered his resignation at Nowata, and the school board reluctantly accepted, but they knew it was inevitable. After Bailey's squad knocked off Dewey, Sallisaw and Lindsey for the 2A state title, the town knew Bailey would be gone, and Sapulpa was the likely candidate.

He resigned with mixed feelings but thought the move up was best for his family and his professional career.

He told the Nowata Star: "This is an extremely difficult decision that I have made. Rarely does a coach have all the advantages in facilities, cooperation and support that I have enjoyed here. The success that we have had could not have occurred except for the faith in the coaches displayed by the administration. We were able to direct our program almost entirely. What an advantage this is for a coach.

"I have the feeling that any decision I make may be wrong, however my ambitions in my profession are such that I cannot do otherwise.

I assure you that I will be a salesman for Nowata and NHS wherever and whenever the opportunity occurs."

Bailey wasn't seen as a deserter or a traitor. High School football coaches are fierce competitors, and they usually don't stay in a single town for too long, especially if it's a small town. Coaches want to try their luck in the bigger classes and sometimes Class 2A just isn't big enough -- even after a state title. Bailey was the only coach in the school's history to hoist the state football trophy, and it was understood that it was time for him to move on.

CHAPTER FIFTEEN
The Girl Scout Murders

A month before Reagor's trial was to begin, the state of Oklahoma was shocked by the worst crime to ever happen up until that time. If the murder of Jerry Bailey replaced the "Porn Wars" as the top story in the local papers, the Girl Scout Murders would push Bailey's murder to the inside of the paper. The Girl Scout Murders would become the biggest story, locally and nationally.

On Monday, June 12, 1977, three Girl Scouts were found raped and beaten to death at Camp Scott near Locust Grove, Oklahoma, located 50 miles east of Tulsa towards Arkansas. Camp Scott was a Girl Scout camp that sat on 400 acres near the foothills of the Ozark Mountains. The camp was surrounded by deep wilderness that could allow the girls to explore, create adventures and make life-long friends.

Several buses loaded with eager campers traveled down Cookie Trail that led to the camp. Some girls couldn't wait to get to camp, but others were apprehensive about leaving their parents for the first time. When the girls arrived, they were split up into several different units designated by Indian names.

Lorilee Farmer, 8, Michelle Guse, 9 and Denise Milner, 10, were selected to the Kiowa Unit and were sent to Tent 8.

The Kiowa Unit was on the outer edge of the camp, and Tent 8 was the farthest and most isolated from the camp. After the girls had arrived and settled in, the camp counselors ordered them to go to bed because of the big day ahead of them. After lights out, laugher and whispering could be heard in almost every tent and the girls were getting to know their tent-mates even though they were supposed to be sleeping.

At midnight, camp counselor Carla Wilhite was awoken by a strange sound in the woods and went outside to take a look. She noticed the sound was coming from near Tent 8, and it didn't seem human. Other girls could hear, what sounded like, a girl crying for her mother. On the first night, the sound of crying wasn't unusual but generally subsided by the second night.

A low-guttural moaning was heard, and it sounded more animal than human. The sound was in fact human. Wilhite's alarm went off early Monday morning, and she wanted to get to the showers so she could have some hot water before the other counselors used all of it. The morning was humid and the ground was still wet from a light rain. Wilhite was walking on the road when she noticed two sleeping bags off to the side. She could see the body of little girl on the ground, and the girl was motionless.

Why would the girls have left their tent to sleep outside? Did a wild animal carry the girls out of the tent? Why didn't the girls scream for help if there was trouble?

Horrified, Wilhite told camp director Barbara Day of her find, and the director made several phone calls, including a call for an ambulance. Day said there were three dead bodies at the camp. At that point, no one knew if the girls were killed by a person or by a wild animal, but they were dead, and the camp was about to be turned into a zoo, buzzing with police officers, detectives and news crews.

The Oklahoma State Bureau of Investigation headed the investigation with help from surrounding law enforcement agencies. Officers from nearby Tahlequah and Tulsa were also dispatched to the scene. It became obvious to investigators that an animal wasn't to blame because the hooks on the back of Tent 8 had been disconnected, and the killer had tried to clean the blood with towels and sheets. The clean-up was apparently a task too daunting for the killer. Blood was splattered on the walls and the floor, and the killer couldn't have cleaned the tent before the morning, so he abandoned the attempt. Investigators believed the girls had been killed inside the tent and dragged several yards away, where they were sexually assaulted.

The killer placed the bloody rags, towels and sheets in the sleeping bags with the girls. The three were bound and gagged with rope, duct tape and carefully sown gags. Reading glasses had also been taken from several tents and discarded as if the killer was trying to find the right prescription. A flashlight had also been left behind.

A search of the area was conducted, and a cave was found that had a camp fire still smoldering. Someone had been there recently, but they were nowhere to be found. It was as if they had vanished into thin air. Tape matching the duct tape used to bind the girls was found in the cave, and newspaper used in the flashlight and several pictures of women were also found.

The pictures found were later published in a local newspaper, and the warden of Granite Reformatory recognized one of the women. A prison officer had moonlighted as a wedding photographer, and a former inmate of the jail had developed the pictures. The killer had planned and committed the murders to near perfection.

Gene Leroy Hart, football star, convicted rapist, burglar, and escaped convict was looking like the kind of person that could do such a thing. Hart was convicted of the rapes of two pregnant women in 1966. He kidnapped the women at gunpoint, put them in the trunk of his car, bound them with nylon rope and duct tape and raped and sodomized them. Hart also took one of his victim's prescription glasses.

One of the rape victims said that Hart made guttural moaning sounds while he raped her. She described the sounds the same way Wilhite had described what she had heard coming from Tent 8 on the night of the murders.

The two women remembered his license tag number, and Hart was quickly apprehended by police. Shortly after, he confessed to raping the two women and was sentenced to three, 10-year sentences. Unbelievably, he was paroled two years and four months later.

Three months after his parole for the rapes, he was then arrested again for burglary and sentenced to 275 years in prison but escaped twice while being housed in the Mayes County Jail. He was recaptured the first time, but the second time he vanished into the thick woods of the Ozark Mountains near Locust Grove, staying hidden for several years.

Hart didn't accomplish his disappearing act on his own. Friends and family helped hide the rapist even though he pleaded guilty to the crime. Local Native Americans and faithful followers of Locust Grove football couldn't believe that Hart could do such a thing, and rumors spread quickly that he was set up by law enforcement.

Townspeople said that Hart could be seen on any given day, fishing, hunting or walking down the street. He used a cave called Goat's Bluff, near Tahlequah, to hide some of the time and it later became a popular hangout for college kids from nearby Northeastern State University.

Local newspapers began running stories about Gene Hart the football hero, not Gene Hart the convicted rapist. O.S.B.I. agents received a tip as to Hart's whereabouts, and they converged on the rundown cabin in the thick woods of the Cookson Hills. A portly-sized Hart attempted to run out the front door of the house, but was met by agents with guns drawn, and he surrendered without incident. Hart was wearing a blue and white striped tank top t-shirt and women's prescription eye glasses he had obviously stolen.

A sample of Hart's hair matched a hair found on the tape used to bind Denise Milner's hands, and a sperm sample was also taken from him and was so unusual it could be used to possibly link him to the murders.

The Locust Grove community held barbeques and fundraisers to raise money for the Gene Leroy Hart

Defense Fund, and the people of the small town began to rally around their "football hero." The Native American community had a profound distrust of the white man's law and felt one of their own was being railroaded. According to that logic, he could rape two pregnant women and leave them to die, but he could never rape and kill three little girls.

Hart was tried and found "not guilty" by a jury of his peers in the Mayes County Courthouse. Those same peers had already decided his innocence before the trial even started, referring to him as 'Ole Gene.' Despite his victory, Hart still needed to finish his almost 300-year prison sentence for rape and burglary.

Hart died in prison of a massive heart attack while jogging. It is said that he used Indian Medicine to deceive, and the only punishment is death. To this day, the case remains open, but the law enforcement agencies that hunted the murderer feel that the right man was charged with the crime.

CHAPTER SIXTEEN
Pretrial Hearing

The hunt for Gene Leroy Hart started while Truster was preparing for his case against Reagor. The media hype had shifted from Reagor to Hart, but the assistant district attorney didn't even notice.

"I never gave a flip about high-profile cases," Truster said. "They are all high-profile to me. As a district attorney, you have to have a sense of the media, and you have to double the effort not to make mistakes. Like when you're on a break during the trial, or just talking to people in general. I never gave it much thought. My only concern was getting a conviction in this case."

There were several preliminary hearings and one, in particular, was the only time Reagor spoke under oath. He never took the stand during the criminal trial but answered questions as to his medication during a hearing on Friday, Dec. 11, 1976 – more than 10 months after the murder. The hearing was to decide if Reagor was competent to stand trial, and the defense was also attempting to suppress Reagor's numerous confessions, citing the U.S. Supreme Court Case of "Simmons vs. United States (1968)."

Judge Margaret Lamm presided over the hearing and Don Gasaway spoke for the defense and Jerry Truster for the prosecution. Reagor was out of jail on bond and traveling back and forth from Sapulpa to Tulsa to receive medication and mental health treatment.

Pretrial Hearing Dec. 11, 1976

JUDGE LAMM: We set the trial on January the 18th at 9:30 a.m.

TRUSTER: Your Honor, I don't have any great quarrel, insofar as what the Court has indicated. I would simply note that we suggested, on behalf of the State, that an earlier trial date be had.

LAMM: Well, because of Mr. Gasaway's schedule, because that's the last week of that jury term, I would put it over to the eighteenth (of January, 1977.)

TRUSTER: Very well, Very well. Would Your Honor wish to proceed on the motion to produce?

LAMM: I thought I might inquire of the defendant if he would come around, please. Mr. Reagor, hold up your right hand, please. Do you solemnly swear the testimony you are about to give will be true and correct, so help you God?

REAGOR: I do.

LAMM: Would you tell me your name, please.

REAGOR: Paul Reagor, Jr.

LAMM: Do you know why you are here?

REAGOR: Yes.

LAMM: Why are you here?

REAGOR: I'm charged with second degree murder.

LAMM: You are taking medication, I understand.

REAGOR: Yes.

LAMM: How often do you take the medication? Four times a day? And, has that enabled you to communicate with your attorney?

REAGOR: Yes.

LAMM: You understand what he tells you and he understands what you tell him?

REAGOR: Yes.

LAMM: Do you have any problem with that at all?

REAGOR: No.

LAMM: Do you know what date today is?

REAGOR: The date?

LAMM: Yes.

REAGOR: December 11th.

LAMM: Do you know the day of the week?

REAGOR: It's Friday.

LAMM: And, what did you have to eat this morning?

REAGOR: Sausage, bread, coffee.

LAMM: As long as you take your medication, are you getting along all right?

REAGOR: Yes. I get along a lot better than I used to.

LAMM: What happens, have you missed any medication at all?

REAGOR: One time, that I can remember missing.

LAMM: And, what happened when you missed taking your medication?

REAGOR: You mean why I missed?

GASAWAY: What happened, Paul, when you missed?

LAMM: What happened?

REAGOR: Well, my head started hurting pretty bad and I got a little dizzy.

LAMM: You don't have any trouble talking with Mr. Heaver or Mr. Gasaway?

REAGOR: No.

LAMM: All right, do you wish to ask him anything?

GASAWAY: I have no questions.

TRUSTER: I would like to inquire briefly under the Simmons decision. Mr. Reagor, do you know a Dr. Edward Norfleet?

REAGOR: Yes.

TRUSTER: Have you seen him?

REAGOR: Yes.

TRUSTER: Has he prescribed medication for you?

REAGOR: No.

TRUSTER: He has not?

REAGOR: No.

TRUSTER: Did you advise Dr. Norfleet of medication that you were taking?

REAGOR: Yes.

TRUSTER: What medication are you taking, sir?

REAGOR: I'm taking Triavil 4.25.

TRUSTER: Milligrams?

REAGOR: I think so.

TRUSTER: Are you taking any additional medication?

REAGOR: No.

TRUSTER: You are seeing Dr. Norfleet, then, apart from the medication that was prescribed for you by someone else, is that right?

REAGOR: Yes.

TRUSTER: Mr. Reagor, are you seeing any other physician?

REAGOR: Well, I go to an outpatient clinic here in Tulsa, Eastern State. They have a branch here.

TRUSTER: For what purpose do you go to that location?

REAGOR: Well, I go there and -- this is where I go to get my medication.

TRUSTER: And, the medication again is what you previously indicated for her honor -- that medication?

REAGOR: Yes.

LAMM: Do you receive or are you taking any other medication prescribed by Eastern State Hospital other than Triavil?

REAGOR: No.

TRUSTER: Upon your visit to the outpatient clinic from Eastern State Hospital where is that located, by the way, please, sir?

REAGOR: It's on Country Club Drive -- Country Club Road, something like that.

TRUSTER: Do you likewise receive any treatment from those individuals at the outpatient clinic in addition to the medication you obtain from them?

GASAWAY: Object, Your Honor, that's a broad statement and a statement of psychiatric nature and could be -- that would be treatment, and he's not competent on that.

LAMM: I think he can say what else happens up there.

GASAWAY: Well, if the question is phrased that way, I wouldn't object.

TRUSTER: Let me ask you, sir, do you know what the term counseling means -- psychiatric counseling?

REAGOR: Not fully. I think I have a general understanding.

TRUSTER: Your general understanding, would you say that is what you are receiving from Dr. Norfleet?

REAGOR: Yes.

TRUSTER: Have you received psychiatric counseling from any member of the outpatient clinic at Eastern State Hospital on Country Club Road?

REAGOR: Yes.

TRUSTER: From whom, and what doctors?

REAGOR: I talked to Dr. Hornicek.

TRUSTER: Dr. Hornicek?

REAGOR: Yes.

TRUSTER: Are you continuing to talk to Dr. Hornicek?

REAGOR: Yes.

TRUSTER: Who else, please, sir?

REAGOR: Well, he's the only one I've talked to. Well, Dr. Ellis.

TRUSTER: Dr. Ellis?

REAGOR: Yes

TRUSTER: Is he located at that facility?

REAGOR: Yes, he is.

TRUSTER: Where is Dr. Norfleet's office, please sir?

REAGOR: It's in the Doctor's Building, across from St. Johns Hospital.

TRUSTER: Have you had interviews or psychiatric counseling under your general understanding of that term, with any other doctors at the outpatient clinic other than Dr. Hornicek or Dr. Ellis?

REAGOR: No.

TRUSTER: During this period of time, Mr. Reagor, that you have been out on bond and taking this medication, have you received psychiatric counseling, under your understanding of that term, or visitations with any other doctors that you have named other than Dr. Hornicek, Dr. Ellis, and Dr. Norfleet?

REAGOR: No.

TRUSTER: Have you ever seen a person by the name Dr. Lynwood Heaver?

GASAWAY: I object to that, your honor. He's already answered the question.

LAMM: He answered that he hadn't seen any other.

GASAWAY: That's right.

TRUSTER: You've never seen any additional doctors?

REAGOR: No.

TRUSTER: Have you ever seen any psychologists opposed to psychiatrist?

GASAWAY: Your honor, I would object. This is going beyond this. I don't see what materiality it has as to whether or not he is in a position to stand trial as contemplated by the court putting him on the witness stand.

TRUSTER: Let me ask this question. Do you know the difference between a psychologist and a psychiatrist?

GASAWAY: Object – not material.

LAMM: Sustained.

TRUSTER: Have you ever seen a Dr. Salvatore Russo?

GASAWAY: Object -- It's been asked and answered three times now.

LAMM: I think he can answer that.

TRUSTER: Have you ever seen a Dr. Salvatore Russo, psychologist?

REAGOR: Not that I know.

TRUSTER: Is that – No, you haven't seen him, or no you are sure you haven't seen him?

GASAWAY: The answer stands for itself. He says "no."

TRUSTER: I would like counsel to take the witness stand to ask who he's seen while out on bond. You have no difficulty do you, Mr. Reagor.

REAGOR: No.

TRUSTER: Do you know what the punishment is for murder in the second decree?

GASAWAY: Object -- immaterial.

LAMM: Sustained.

TRUSTER: Have you had any difficulty today or, any time up to today, within the last week or ten days, communicating with your attorneys?

REAGOR: No.

TRUSTER: Do you have any difficulty communicating with your family?

REAGOR: No.

TRUSTER: You indicated that your head hurt when you did not take the medication, Triavil, in that correct? You get dizzy?

REAGOR: Yes.

TRUSTER: What day did you not take the medication, please, sir?

REAGOR: Thanksgiving Day.

TRUSTER: Have you ever missed any other days since you've been out on bond in taking the medication, Triavil?

REAGOR: No, I haven't.

TRUSTER: And you take it religiously, four times a day, is that correct?

REAGOR: I don't religiously, but I take it four times a day.

TRUSTER: Do you follow your doctor's advice in taking it four times a day or don't you?

REAGOR: Yes, I do.

TRUSTER: Now, Mr. Reagor, is there anything about the immediate effects of taking that medication that causes you any difficulty to know of your own surroundings or the presence of people or ability to communicate with individuals?

GASAWAY: Your Honor, we would object to it. This is going too far outside the scope of Simmons. I think the court has got an opinion to this point whether or not Mr. Reagor should stand trial. I think Mr. Truster is trying to depose it and it doesn't make any difference.

TRUSTER: Yes, it does, at the time of trial. The Court has not touched on that line of inquiry at this time. If this man, after taking medication, has ill effects, something that would prevent him from standing trial, understanding the nature of the witnesses proceeding to testify against him, I think that is a proper inquiry. I have that question and no others.

LAMM: I think he can answer that.

TRUSTER: Do you have any side effects, anything at all, Mr. Reagor, after you take the medication that somehow puts you in a disability to communicate with people or understand the nature of your surroundings, anything at all of that nature?

REAGOR: No.

TRUSTER: You are fully aware, then, after you take that medication, four times a day, of exactly what happened?

REAGOR: Yes.

TRUSTER: Thank you. No further questions.

GASAWAY: Just -- you see Dr. Norfleet at your own volition, do you not?

REAGOR: Yes, now I do.

GASAWAY: Also see him because the court directed you to, do you not?

REAGOR: Yes.

GASAWAY: You are doing exactly what the court ordered you to do, aren't you?

REAGOR: Yes.

GASAWAY: That's all.

Judge Lamm then set a trial date for January 24, 1977. However, Reagor was sent back to the hospital after another "spell," and the trial date had to be moved back. He was readmitted to Eastern State Hospital on Jan. 21, 1977 –

three days before his trial – and during the 60 day period he was deemed unable to distinguish from right and wrong and unable to assist in his own defense. He was discharged on Feb. 24, 1977 but readmitted a day later on Feb. 25.

During that 60-day observation period, Reagor was found sane and able to assist in his defense and was discharged on April 19, 1977. The trial was then set for early July and this time, Reagor would stand trial for second degree murder.

CHAPTER SEVENTEEN
The trial

The trial of Paul Reagor Jr. vs. The State of Oklahoma (CS-76-220) began on July 11, 1977 on the sixth floor of the Tulsa County Courthouse before the honorable Judge Margaret Lamm.

Judge Lamm was a matronly, kind woman that was known for being fair to both the prosecution as well as the defense. She allowed the cases to be tried by the lawyers and gave both sides equal amount of leeway. Her rulings were practical and fair to both sides, and she was well respected by both the prosecution and defense attorneys. The judge was 70 years old, with brown hair and a round face that was always seemed to wear a smile.

She was born April 29, 1907, in Grand Junction, Colorado. She graduated from the University of Tulsa law school in 1944 and became Tulsa's first woman assistant county attorney in 1947. During that time, Lamm was a proponent of finding fathers who failed to provide for their children and filed cases against the deadbeat dads.

In September of 1972 she became Oklahoma's first woman to be appointed a full district judge by a governor (Gov. David Hall). Three years later, in 1975, the judge made headlines again when she disqualified herself from hearing a lawsuit the Fraternal Order of Police had filed against Tulsa Mayor Robert J. LaFortune. She had signed the FOP's charter change petition and told the court she sympathized with the officers. She retired from the bench on Jan. 31, 1985.

The first four days consisted of jury selection, but the trial testimony didn't start until July 15, and the jury was sworn in, sequestered and voir dired, individually.

Voir diring the jury individually was usually a defensive strategy and a way for attorneys to find out whether a potential juror had any knowledge of the case or if they had already decided the defendant's guilt or innocence. However, it was Truster that wanted to make sure the jury didn't have any pre-conceived notions about Reagor's innocence or guilt and didn't want to give the defense anything that could overturn what he hoped would be a guilty verdict.

Fourteen jurors were selected, eight women and six men, 12 jurors and two alternates: Ellen Levy, Maxine Glasby, Paul L. Harrison, Georgette T. Stockdale, Barbara Scott, Norman J. Nelson, M.R. Small, Marcella Lee Johnson, John Stephen Nichols, Glenn Chowins, Patricia Dennis, Rebecca Sue Stephens, Nancy S. Ferguson and Robert Carson Todd.

The case had received significant press coverage in print, radio and on television, and all three local TV news stations (KTUL-ABC, KJRH- NBC, KOTV- CBS) followed the crime and trial closely, as well as the Sapulpa Daily Herald, The Tulsa Tribune, Tulsa World and Nowata Daily Star newspapers. All of the news outlets covered the case from the day the two coaches were missing and also reported on trial testimony, trial motions and the verdict.

The press coverage concerned both the prosecution and the defense teams, and the jury was sequestered in a downtown Tulsa hotel that wasn't too far from the court house. Reagor was still free on the $35,000 bond and hadn't spent a day in jail due to the constant hospital stays and the insanity defense strategy.

The trial testimony started four days after jury selection started on July 15, 1977, and the prosecution called Jerry Bailey's wife, Beverly Bailey, to the stand to testify first.

Direct examination of Beverly Bailey by assistant district attorney Jerry Truster:

TRUSTER: Would you state your name for the Court and members of the jury, please, ma'am.

BAILEY: My name is Beverly Bailey.

TRUSTER: And, I'll ask you what is your business, profession or occupation?

BAILEY: I'm a school teacher.

TRUSTER: And, for whom are you employed?

BAILEY: I'm employed for the Sapulpa Public School System.

TRUSTER: Do you teach a particular grade, Beverly?

BAILEY: Yes. I teach in the high school.

TRUSTER: Any particular subject?

BAILEY: I teach mathematics.

TRUSTER: Were you so employed in that capacity on January 22nd, 1976?

BAILEY: Yes, I was.

TRUSTER: And, were you teaching on that date, please, ma 'am?

BAILEY: Yes, sir.

TRUSTER: And, now, you are the widow of Jerry Bailey?

BAILEY: Yes.

TRUSTER: Do you have children?

BAILEY: I have two.

TRUSTER: And, what are their names?

BAILEY: My son is Guy Bailey and my daughter is Diedra Bailey.

TRUSTER: And, how old is Guy?

BAILEY: Guy is fourteen.

TRUSTER: And, how about Diedra?

BAILEY: She's thirteen.

TRUSTER: Directing your attention to Thursday morning, 1976, January the 22nd, I'll ask you if you had occasion to go to school that day.

BAILEY: Yes, I did.

TRUSTER: And, did you go there by yourself?

BAILEY: No, I did not. I took my daughter to school.

TRUSTER: What time did you get to the high school?

BAILEY: I got in the school about 7:30 that morning.

TRUSTER: All right, and, what did you do upon arrival there?

BAILEY: I went to check in, and the front door of the main office was locked, and I had to go through the attendance office to check in and get my attendance papers and bulletins for the day.

TRUSTER: All right, was there any other persons likewise that arrived about that time or was in the office on that occasion?

BAILEY: The only one I noticed in the office at that time was Hazel Smith. She was in the attendance office when I went through.

TRUSTER: All right, and, do you know a person by the name of Paul Reagor, Jr.?

BAILEY: Yes, I do.

TRUSTER: And, in what way did you know Paul Reagor, Jr. at this time of January the 22nd, 1976?

BAILEY: At that time he was my vice principal in charge of attendance.

TRUSTER: Did you have occasion to see him that morning as you testified that you went into the office?

BAILEY: The first time I was in the office, no. Later on I did, yes.

TRUSTER: About what time did you see him first, Beverly?

BAILEY: I was back in the attendance office at approximately fifteen (minutes) till eight, checking on attendance matters. He walked into the office.

TRUSTER: Did you have conversation with Mr. Reagor at that time?

BAILEY: No, I did not.

TRUSTER: Did anyone in your presence and in the presence of Mr. Reagor?

BAILEY: Yes.

TRUSTER: And, what was said?

BAILEY: Hazel Smith, the attendance clerk asked him why he was at school so early.

TRUSTER: Did he respond in your presence?

BAILEY: No, he did not.

TRUSTER: Why he was at school so early?

BAILEY: No.

TRUSTER: That was what was said, Why was he at school so early?

BAILEY: Uh-huh.

TRUSTER: Now, Beverly, Jerry was the head football coach, was he not?

BAILEY: Yes, he was.

TRUSTER: Was he employed in that capacity on January the 22nd, 1976?

BAILEY: No, he was not. He had resigned his head coaching position.

TRUSTER: And, how about the defendant Paul Reagor, Jr was he in any way connected with your husband in the coaching aspect?

BAILEY: Well, he had been his assistant.

TRUSTER: For how long?

BAILEY: For the 1975 football season.

TRUSTER: All right, which is the season just concluded before this date in January, 1975?

BAILEY: Yes.

TRUSTER: Did Jerry resign?

BAILEY: Yes, he did.

TRUSTER: When did he resign his position as head football coach?

BAILEY: On December the 8th, 1976.

TRUSTER: Now, Beverly, do you have knowledge, ma'am, insofar as any applicants for Jerry's position or anything specifically in regards to the defendant, Paul Reagor, Jr.?

BAILEY: The only thing that I know in reference to this is the fact that at the time of my husband's resignation, the papers said —

GASAWAY: Object, Your Honor, to what was quoted.

JUDGE LAMM: Sustained.

TRUSTER: Let me ask you this, was it common knowledge whether or not Paul Reagor was going to apply for -- sought the head coaching job?

GASAWAY: Excuse me. Object to that, Your Honor.

JUDGE LAMM: Sustained.

TRUSTER: Beverly, had a coach been selected sometime before January the 22nd, 1976 to fill the position that your husband held?

BAILEY Yes.

TRUSTER: And, who was that person by name?

BAILEY: His name was Art Davis. He's head coach there now.

TRUSTER: All right, do you know of your own knowledge whether or not any interviews were held for applicants insofar as the head coaching job is concerned?

BAILEY: I do know that the assistant coaches --

GASAWAY: We object. It can be answered yes or no.

THE COURT: Answer it, yes or no.

BAILEY: Yes.

TRUSTER: Yes, you have knowledge, in what way?

BAILEY: I do know that the assistant coaches were talked to in regard to the job. What was said or anything, I do not know. I just know they were interviewed.

TRUSTER: I understand. Was Mr. Paul Reagor, Jr., to your knowledge, interviewed likewise, he being an assistant coach?

BAILEY: Yes, he was.

TRUSTER: All right, now, Beverly, insofar as you seeing Mr. Reagor in the office earlier, when was the first time that you became aware on Thursday, January the 22nd that your husband had not been in class that morning?

BAILEY: My first awareness that he was not in class was at the beginning of our second hour which is approximately 9:30 a.m. A student that I had in my second hour class, that was in my husband's first hour class, asked me why he wasn't in class.

TRUSTER: What did you say or do in response to that?

BAILEY: At that time I went to the nearest telephone and I called the house and I got no answer.

TRUSTER: Now, you had left earlier, leaving behind Guy and Jerry at your home?

BAILEY: Yes.

TRUSTER: Okay. Now, what did you then do, Beverly?

BAILEY: I went back to my classroom and about midway through second hour, I heard a commotion next door and I stepped out in the hall to see if the teacher next door might be having a problem, and she was not, and while I was out in the hall, I went to my husband's classroom to see if he was there. When I stepped in the doorway, one of his football players and also one of my students asked me where Coach was. I just responded with a shrug of my shoulders.

TRUSTER: Okay, and, at that point, you still did not know?

BAILEY: Right.

TRUSTER: Okay. When were you made aware that day that something was amiss or the fact that Jerry was not in school at all and deemed to be missing?

BAILEY: The assistant principal in charge of discipline, Ron James, came to my classroom shortly after third hour had started, which starts at 10:30 a.m. and asked me where my husband was. I said I did not know and asked if he wasn't in the office with him, and he told me, no, and that a policeman wanted to see me and would I please come to the office. In route to the office, he told me that my husband was missing, and they had found some of his papers near Bixby.

TRUSTER: All right, you never did see Jerry any more that time you left him at home?

BAILEY: No, I didn't

TRUSTER: Where your husband was?

BAILEY: Right.

TRUSTER: Did you seek to locate him further, based upon those things that you were now aware of?

BAILEY: No, I did not. On other occasions, he had been called to the office to help with problems that might be going on between parents and students, and I assumed that he was probably in the office, and I did not go to the office to check.

TRUSTER: Ma'am, are you familiar with the kind of car that Paul Reagor drives or was driving at that time?

BAILEY: No.

TRUSTER: You were not? All right. Now, did Guy have a basketball game that evening?

BAILEY: Yes, he did.

TRUSTER: And, this was Thursday, January 22nd I'm speaking of.

BAILEY: Yes, it is.

TRUSTER: Was it customary for Jerry to attend Guy's basketball games in the evening?

BAILEY: He was usually able to attend his basketball games unless he had to help with a wrestling match or basketball game in some capacity. He tried to attend as many as he could. He was planning on attending that game.

TRUSTER: Thank you, Beverly. No more questions. They will have some questions.

Cross examination by defense attorney Don E. Gasaway

GASAWAY: Mrs. Bailey, do you know what position Mr. Reagor filled at the school at that time?

161

BAILEY: To my knowledge at that time he was vice principal, and I did not know at that time that he resigned. I still thought he was assistant football coach.

GASAWAY: Now, is a vice principal commonly called an administrative position?

BAILEY: Yes, it is.

GASAWAY: Does that pay more than a coaching position, if you know?

BAILEY: I don't really know. I would assume, but I don't know.

GASAWAY: Well, in your opinion, as a school teacher, would that be a job that most people strive for in school business?

BAILEY: A lot of times a teacher will go from a teaching position to an administrative position.

GASAWAY: Now, are you aware of any recommendations Mr. Bailey may have made in regard to the coaching position?

BAILEY: Yes, I am.

GASAWAY: Are you aware that he recommended Mr. Reagor?

BAILEY: Yes, I am.

GASAWAY: Okay. That's all we have, Your Honor.

TRUSTER: Nothing further, Your Honor.

JUDGE LAMM: Thank you, Mrs. Bailey.

Beverly Bailey was excused from the stand. She was a little shaken but was a great witness for the prosecution. She had just testified against the man that killed her husband, showing grace and poise.

The prosecution then called Guy Bailey to the stand. Guy was now 14 years old and going into the ninth grade at the Sapulpa Junior High. It had been 16 months since the murder of his father, and he was one of the last people to see him alive. He was also one of the last people to see his father and Reagor together.

Direct examination of Guy Bailey by Assistant DA Jerry Truster

JUDGE LAMM: Call your next witness, please.

TRUSTER: Guy Bailey.

THE COURT: Do you solemnly swear the testimony you are about to give in the matter now on trial, will be the truth, the whole truth, and nothing but the truth, so help you God?

GUY BAILEY: Yes.

TRUSTER: State your name, please.

GUY BAILEY: Guy Bailey.

TRUSTER: How old are you, Guy?

GUY BAILEY: Fourteen.

TRUSTER: Do you go to school?

GUY BAILEY: Yes.

TRUSTER: Where?

GUY BAILEY: Sapulpa Junior High.

TRUSTER: And, what grade are you going to be in this next fall?

GUY BAILEY: Ninth.

TRUSTER: Guy, getting back to about eighteen months ago, January the 22nd, a Thursday, 1976, do you recall going to school with your dad that day?

GUY BAILEY: Yes.

TRUSTER: Okay, will you tell the members of the jury about the things that occurred leading up to your dad taking you to school that morning.

GUY BAILEY: Well, we got up, and it was normal for me to get up and I'd get up before he did because he would lie in bed for a while. I would usually get ready before he would. I would bring up his coffee, and he'd drink the coffee and get dressed and get his shoes on, and we'd take off.

TRUSTER: Okay. What time did you take off that morning on that Thursday, if you recall?

GUY BAILEY: About ten (minutes) after eight.

TRUSTER: And, how long did it take you to get from your house to Sapulpa High School or Junior High?

GUY BAILEY: Approximately, about five minutes.

TRUSTER: All right. Where did you park, Guy?

GUY BAILEY: In the back parking lot near the facility.

TRUSTER: The new facility? What facility is that?

GUY BAILEY: Sports. It's for the outdoor dressing room.

TRUSTER: Okay. Did you pretty much go to school with your dad every morning?

GUY BAILEY: Most every morning.

TRUSTER: Did you pretty much park in the same place most every morning?

GUY BAILEY: We usually parked in the exact same place every morning.

TRUSTER: Now, Guy, that day, did you have any basketball game that you were playing in that evening?

GUY BAILEY: Yes.

TRUSTER: And, did you and your dad have any conversation concerning the playing of that basketball game later in the day?

GUY BAILEY: That's mainly what we talked about on the way to school. He was telling me a few pointers on what I should do to improve what I was going to do, and I was expecting him to be there.

TRUSTER: Tell the members of the jury what happened when you got to the facility where you and your dad parked.

GUY BAILEY: We parked. He got his clipboard and put his keys under the mat. We both got out and started toward the school.

TRUSTER: All right, now, you say his clipboard. Did he have some papers with him?

GUY BAILEY: Yes. He was planning to get another job. He had job applications for another town to be a coach or a teacher or something like that. He had those on his clipboard.

TRUSTER: Okay, now, did you see -- do you know Paul Reagor, Jr.?

GUY BAILEY: Yes.

TRUSTER: Do you see him present today?

GUY BAILEY: Yes.

TRUSTER: Did you know him back in January 22nd, 1976?

GUY BAILEY: Yes.

TRUSTER: Did you see Mr. Reagor come outside from the area of the school that morning when you arrived there with your dad?

GUY BAILEY: Yes, I did.

TRUSTER: Tell the members of the jury about that, Guy.

GUY BAILEY: Well, we were just starting -- we had just got out of the pickup and started going towards the school. He came in between the two cars and started out towards us. He asked me how I was doing that morning. I told him just fine. I was kind of in a hurry to get to school. I heard just a few things. He started talking to my dad. He was pretty near. He was asking what kind of work he was going to do now that he resigned.

TRUSTER: Words to that effect?

GUY BAILEY: Yes.

TRUSTER: You didn't stay there and listen to the exact conversation?

GUY BAILEY: No. I was in a hurry.

TRUSTER: Wanted to get to class?

GUY BAILEY: Yes.

TRUSTER: Did you see your dad or Mr. Reagor leave at any time? Did you look back and see them get into anybody's car?

GUY BAILEY: No. After probably half-way there I kind of started walking pretty fast -- kind of running because class started in about ten minutes.

TRUSTER: Okay. No further questions. Thank you. They will have some questions. Thank you, Guy.

Cross examination by defense attorney Don Gasaway

GASAWAY: Guy, what keys do you remember your dad putting under the mat, if you remember?

GUY BAILEY: Car keys, usually. (He) just placed them under the mat or under the seat.

GASAWAY: All right, sir, now, do you recall when you first learned that your father was missing?

GUY BAILEY: I'm not sure. I think it was lunch period.

GASAWAY: All right, do you know if his truck was still in the parking lot at that time?

GUY BAILEY: I didn't go out and check.

GASAWAY: Did you subsequently determine or find out that the car was there?

GUY BAILEY: I didn't find out where the pickup was until later on that evening. My mother told me at home.

GASAWAY: Was it still in the parking lot?

GUY BAILEY: I think they took it somewhere. I have no idea.

GASAWAY: Do you know how many sets of keys your father had for that pickup?

GUY BAILEY: He had two.

GASAWAY: Two sets? Did he always carry both sets of keys with him?

GUY BAILEY: No, he left one at home for my mother.

GASAWAY: So, he only placed one set of keys under the floor mat?

GUY BAILEY: Yes.

GASAWAY: Nothing further.

TRUSTER: No further questions.

THE COURT: Thank you.

Guy Bailey was then excused from the stand. At age 14, he was technically still a boy, but he seemed more like a grown man while testifying against the man that murdered his dad.

The prosecution then called wrestling head coach Steve Shibley to the stand.

Shibley testified to seeing Bailey and Reagor, in Reagor's car, heading out of town on the morning of the murder.

"I was late for school about somewhere between 8:10 and 8:15 a.m. I was in a hurry and I was at a stop sign on the way to the high school. Directly across the street, I saw Paul Reagor's car across from me," Shibley said.

He said that two coaches were heading north out of town towards Tulsa, and the two men acknowledged him.

Truster asked Shibley if he saw Bailey or Reagor at any other time of the day and he said "No."

Gasaway's cross examination was benign. He asked questions about the hiring of new head football coach, Art Davis, and when it happened. The defense attorney also asked Shibley if the two men looked fine when he saw them in Reagor's car, and he said they did.

During a break in the trial, Shibley was getting on the elevator at the court house. He had just gone outside to smoke a cigarette and needed to get to the court room and wasn't really paying much attention. When the elevator doors opened up he walked in and all of the blood rushed to his head. He saw Reagor standing in the corner of the elevator. Shibley had imagined over and over what he would do if he could be alone with Reagor. Now, he was.

Shibley had already walked onto the elevator, and by the time he realized he didn't want to be on the elevator with Reagor, the doors closed. He had so many questions to ask the man that killed his friend, but he couldn't form the words. His mind was racing and he was mad -- real mad. The tension was thick, and Reagor decided to break the ice.

"How's it going, Shib?" Reagor asked.

"Just fine, Buck," Shibley said, refusing to look at him.

Shibley was so furious that he got off on the wrong floor. He didn't want to be anywhere near the man that killed his friend.

Truster then called former KTUL-TV general assignment reporter Edwin Poston to the stand. Poston was now a vice president at Media Five Inc., a public relations and advertising firm in Tulsa. While on the stand, he recalled his involvement, starting on Thursday, January 22, 1976. He said that his boss granted his request to cover the two missing coaches story. He then talked to one of his sources in the Jenks Police Department and was given the vicinity of the area where the search was being conducted.

The following day, Poston went to the Sapulpa Daily Herald for pictures of the two coaches and to get as much information as he could to help in his story. He then got the description of the car and the tag from the Sapulpa Police Department and headed for the Bixby area.

After driving around Bixby for an hour or so, Poston and his cameraman Red Stattum saw a Medi-vac helicopter, flown by Steve McKim, and flagged them down to get some footage of the area for the news.

They were in the helicopter for around 25 minutes when they spotted a car matching Reagor's description at an abandoned farm house. There were weeds and sunflowers knocked down behind the car as if the car had been there for only a short period of time.

They landed the helicopter around 150 yards from the house in an empty field adjacent to the dwelling.

"We ran up to the car and as soon as we got up to 50-feet or so, we could see it was the car we were looking for," Poston said. "The tag matched and we could see blood on the bumper of the car."

There was no one in the inside of the car and Steve McKim, a Medivac crew member, looked inside of a shed

168

next to the house. The shed was clear and they knew they needed to call the Sheriff's Department. Highway Patrolmen and Sapulpa Police started to arrive a little after noon and began the investigation.

Poston testified that Steve McKim was the first person to enter the house and saw Reagor lying on a mattress in a bed room.

"Steve McKim walked through the screen door and he stepped right back, and he said, 'there is someone in there, and he's breathing.'"

Gasaway then cross examined Poston and asked questions about gravel, dirt and dust on the road leading to the house. He also asked about the initial phase of the investigation. Poston testified that at no time did he enter the house, and he did his best to preserve the crime scene until the police arrived.

Truster then called Tulsa County Sheriff Lt. Robert Randolph to the stand.

The basic questions were asked and answered, but the heart of Randolph's testimony was whether or not Reagor acknowledged and understood his Miranda Rights.

Direct examination of Lt. Robert Randolph by Assistant DA Jerry Truster

TRUSTER: All right, now, sir, tell the court and for the jury exactly what you did upon entering the house.

RANDOLPH: When I entered the house I observed Paul Reagor, Jr. laying in the floor of the kitchen in this area here in the house.

TRUSTER: All right.

RANDOLPH: Immediately upon seeing him, I went to him, advised him of his rights under the Miranda Rule.

TRUSTER: All right, now, you've indicated an individual by the name of Paul Reagor, Jr. Do you see that person present in the Court today?

RANDOLPH: Yes, sir, I do.

TRUSTER: For the record, where is he seated and what is he wearing?

RANDOLPH: A light green shirt, black jacket, sitting at the table with Mr. Gasaway and Mr. Heaver.

JUDGE LAMM: The record would reflect he identified the defendant.

TRUSTER: Thank you very much. You first saw him in the area that you've indicated, and you advised him of his rights pursuant to Miranda Rule. Will you tell the Court, and for the record, please, sir, what specific rights you advised him of?

RANDOLPH: That he had a right to remain silent. That anything he said could be used against him in a court of law. That he had a right to have an attorney present during any questions. That if he didn't have the funds to employ an attorney that the state would furnish one. Also, that he had a right to talk to us about the case, and that he could stop at any time he so wished if he so desired. I asked if he understood his rights, and he indicated that he did.

TRUSTER: All right.

RANDOLPH: By answering: Yes.

TRUSTER: Those were his words?

RANDOLPH: Yes, sir.

TRUSTER: Now, did you read those rights from a card or did you recite them in the manner that you indicated for the members of the jury today?

RANDOLPH: Recited them.

TRUSTER: All right, sir, in what tone of voice did Mr. Reagor use in responding to the Miranda Warning that you gave him, sir?

RANDOLPH: A low, audible voice, barely above a whisper.

TRUSTER: All right, did you have further conversation with him or make any additional statement to him at that time?

RANDOLPH: I asked him if he had shot Bailey and where the gun was. When I asked him if he had shot Bailey, he looked surprised.

GASAWAY: Object to the conclusion and ask it be stricken.

JUDGE LAMM: He can state how he looked.

TRUSTER: He looked surprised?

RANDOLPH: With the expression on his face.

GASAWAY: We object to counsel's leading question.

TRUSTER: He just answered the question. He could testify to what he observed.

JUDGE LAMM: He can testify to what he observed, yes.

GASAWAY: That doesn't give counsel the right to lead him. We object on that basis.

JUDGE LAMM: (To Truster) Don't lead him.

TRUSTER: What do you mean when you say that statement that counsel objected to a minute ago? Describe what action Mr. Reagor took?

RANDOLPH: I feel like when a person -- when you ask them something and they look surprised -- it's just obvious the way the face shows it. They open their eyes wider. To me, it's just obvious.

TRUSTER: Did Mr. Reagor exhibit a facial expression to you?

RANDOLPH: Yes, sir.

TRUSTER: All right, and, based upon the facial expression exhibited to you, you concluded that he appeared to act surprised?

RANDOLPH: Yes.

TRUSTER: Very well. Did you have additional conversation with the defendant?

RANDOLPH: I asked him where the gun was. He said, "What gun?" and at this time the medical personnel were arriving, and the conversation ceased.

TRUSTER: All right, now, the medical personnel that were arriving, sir, who do you mean specifically?

RANDOLPH: The ambulance people from Broken Arrow.

TRUSTER: To your knowledge, did you call or someone call before you went into the house requesting an ambulance to be sent?

RANDOLPH: Well, apparently it had been some time before I arrived there.

TRUSTER: All right, now, who else was in the room with you, please, sir?

RANDOLPH: At this particular time?

TRUSTER: At the very particular time that you advised the defendant of his rights pursuant to the Miranda Warning?

RANDOLPH: Steve McKim, Sergeant Richard Johnson of the Sapulpa Police Department.

TRUSTER: And, where was Mr. Kim and Lieutenant Johnson in relation to where you were?

RANDOLPH: Somewhere behind me.

TRUSTER: I need to ask you this, how close were you to Mr. Reagor as he was lying in this area of the house that you described?

RANDOLPH: He way lying on the floor, and I was kneeling down, up by his head and shoulders. I was facing east. His head would have been facing to the north, and I don't know exactly where McKim was, but Johnson was in this area right here by the door -- hallway area.

TRUSTER: All right, sir, and, you were then in between the defendant who was lying on the floor and Sergeant Richard Johnson of the Sapulpa Police Department?

RANDOLPH: Yes, sir.

TRUSTER: All right, now, when he responded with the words, 'What gun?' were those likewise also barely audible above a whisper?

RANDOLPH: Yes, sir.

TRUSTER: What did you do when the ambulance people from Broken Arrow arrived?

RANDOLPH: They started to load him; I proceeded from that location back to the vehicle.

TRUSTER: All right, and, in respect to the way Mr. Reagor appeared to you on that time that you advised him of the Miranda Rule, I'll hand you what's been marked for identification as State's exhibit No. 14 and ask you to identify that and tell the members of the jury what this is, if you know.

RANDOLPH: This is a picture of Paul Reagor, Jr. shortly after I had talked to him, and he was being loaded to leave the house.

Truster then questioned Randolph about asking Reagor, in the hospital, if he understood the Miranda Warning given to him.

TRUSTER: Were there compartments or partitioned off areas in the emergency room to the left and to the right of Mr. Reagor's section that he was occupying?

RANDOLPH: Yes, there is.

TRUSTER: Was he handcuffed when you observed him seated on the examination table?

RANDOLPH: No, sir, he wasn't.

TRUSTER: He was sitting up at that time?

RANDOLPH: Yes, sir.

TRUSTER: What time of day was this, Bob?

RANDOLPH: Would have been three 3 p.m.

TRUSTER: All right, and, what did you do or say to Mr. Reagor at that time?

RANDOLPH: Immediately, upon walking into this area, I asked him -- I said, "Do you remember me?" He said, "Yes." I said, "Do you remember me advising you of your rights?" He said, "Yes."

TRUSTER: Are these the exact words?

RANDOLPH: Yes, sir.

TRUSTER: All right, did you have further conversation with Mr. Reagor?

RANDOLPH: Yes, sir, I did.

TRUSTER: What took place?

RANDOLPH: I asked him if he killed Jerry Bailey. He said, "Yes."

TRUSTER: Did you have additional conversation?

RANDOLPH: I asked him how he killed him, and he said, "With a butcher knife." I asked him why he killed him, and he said, "Because he had been messing me around." I asked him where he had killed him, and he said, "On Mingo," but didn't know exactly. We talked in areas between 121st and 111th and from the conversation I had with him from where I asked him about throwing some papers -- where some papers were thrown out-- I took it to be somewhere between 121st and 111th.

TRUSTER: Now, could you give your best memory insofar as the exact conversation, question and answer fashion, that you had with Mr. Reagor concerning where he killed Jerry Bailey.

RANDOLPH: He said, "On Mingo." I said, "Where at on Mingo?" He stated then that he didn't know, and so I asked him -- I said, "We found papers yesterday on Mingo around 121st." I said, "Where from there?" He said, "On down the road." By "on down the road," I took it that he meant to the north, which would have been towards 111th.

TRUSTER: All right, sir, now, at that location of on down the road towards 111th Street, is that located in Tulsa County?

RANDOLPH: Yes, sir.

TRUSTER: All right, how about if it was going on down the road south, towards the other direction, would that be likewise in Tulsa County?

RANDOLPH: Just until you get to 211th Street South.

TRUSTER: At that point, is there any other designation or is Mingo Road designated as Mingo Road?

RANDOLPH: From 211th Street South to 76th Street North, north of 76th Street is designated 97th East Avenue.

TRUSTER: All right, so, you have Mingo Road -- that designation applies solely to Tulsa County?

RANDOLPH: To my knowledge, yes, sir.

TRUSTER: Very well. Now, what additional conversation, then, did you have with Mr. Reagor?

RANDOLPH: I asked him how the incident took place. He stated they were driving around, that he pulled up, stopped the car on a little side road off of Mingo. That he handed the keys to Bailey, told him to open the trunk that he had something he wanted to show him. That Bailey got out, went around, and as Bailey got out, he reached under the front seat, got the butcher knife, got out of the car, came around. Just as Bailey opened the trunk and raised up, he said that Bailey asked him, "What's going on?" He replied, "You're the one that's been messing me around." He said he stabbed him. I said, "How many times did you stab him?" He said, "More than once." He then pushed him into the trunk and drove off and went to the location of where he was found and had been there until he had been found from the prior day on a Thursday, sometime in the morning before noon.

TRUSTER: All right, now, Thursday morning before noon is the time in which he told you that he --

RANDOLPH: Yes, No specific time -- only before noon.

TRUSTER: Before noon on Thursday, January the 22nd?

RANDOLPH: Yes, sir.

TRUSTER: All right, sir, did you have any additional conversation with Mr. Reagor at that time?

RANDOLPH: No, sir. I believe that's the conclusion -- most of it.

TRUSTER: Did you have any difficulty understanding the responses given by Mr. Reagor to you -- to your questions?

RANDOLPH: No, sir.

Gasaway then asked Randolph a series of questions, trying to establish shoddy police work. He got Randolph to admit to blood samples hadn't been taken from the car or Reagor's body. Also, the lieutenant wasn't sure if the car was fingerprinted, and Gasaway got him to admit that several people touched the trunk of the car during the investigation. Gasaway also tried to establish that the wrong law enforcement agency was granted jurisdiction.

Gasaway ended his questioning by getting Randolph to admit that no police agency ever found the murder weapon.

Truster then called Sapulpa police officer Richard Johnson to the stand.

Johnson recalled the investigation just as Randolph had except Johnson didn't hear Reagor's affirmation of Randolph's Miranda Warning.

Direct examination of Sgt. Richard Johnson by Assistant DA Truster

TRUSTER: Are you familiar with the Miranda Warning pursuant to the Supreme Court dictates?

JOHNSON: Yes, sir.

TRUSTER: Did you hear the defendant respond in any fashion?

JOHNSON: No, sir. I did not.

TRUSTER: Was Randolph's back to you, sir?

JOHNSON: Yes, sir. It was.

TRUSTER: He was between yourself and the defendant?

JOHNSON: Yes, sir.

Truster then asked about the conversation Johnson and Reagor had in the back of the ambulance where he had admitted to killing Jerry Bailey and throwing the knife out the window. Johnson asked him why he killed Bailey, and Reagor said, "I guess, it was because of the hate."

Gasaway then questioned Officer Johnson and he admitted that he didn't advise Reagor of his Miranda Rights because Randolph told him he had already advised him. The defense attorney also got Officer Johnson to admit that what Reagor did was unusual and abnormal in an attempt to bolster their case of insanity.

Cross examination by defense attorney Gasaway.

GASAWAY: When you investigate a homicide and came upon a suspect, is he normally prone on a mattress?

JOHNSON: No, sir. He is not.

GASAWAY: Would you say that is unusual?

JOHNSON: Yes, sir.

GASAWAY: Would you say that putting somebody in the trunk of a car and driving around was unusual?

JOHNSON: Yes, sir.

GASAWAY: Would you say that it was abnormal?

JOHNSON: It depends on what you mean by abnormal.

GASAWAY: Not normal.

JOHNSON: It's not normal to drive around with a body in the trunk of your car.

The Sapulpa officer then guarded Reagor for about 20 minutes, including the ambulance ride, and handed him over to Officer Whisenhunt at the hospital.

Johnson said, "Deputy Whisenhunt asked if Mr. Reagor had been advised of his rights -- if he understood his rights."

He then said that Reagor nodded his head in affirmation.

Johnson said that his only other conversation with Reagor was when asked for a glass of water.

Truster then called Tulsa County Sheriff's Criminal Investigator Norman Whisenhunt to the stand.

Whisenhunt testified that he asked Reagor if he had been advised of his rights.

"...I asked Mr. Reagor if he had been advised of his rights. He said, 'Yes.' I asked if he understood them and he said, 'Yes.'"

Gasaway asked Whisenhunt if Reagor's fingernail scrapings or the blood on Reagor's shirt had ever been tested, and the officer said that, to his knowledge, they were still in the vault.

Truster then called Tulsa County Medical Examiner Dr. Robert Fogel to the stand.

Fogel was a certified forensic pathologist and worked in that capacity as a consultant pathologist to the State Medical Examiner's Office.

Direct examination of Dr. Robert Fogel by Assistant DA Jerry Truster

TRUSTER: And, in your capacity that you indicated, did you have occasion to conduct an autopsy of one Jerry Bailey?

FOGEL: I did, sir.

TRUSTER: And, where did that take place.

FOGEL: The autopsy was done in the morgue of the State Medical Examiner's Office, Eastern Division, Tulsa, Oklahoma, Southwest Boulevard and 41st Street.

TRUSTER: About what time of day was that done?

FOGEL: 11:45 a.m.

TRUSTER: And, I'll ask you, sir, would you indicate for the members of the jury the results of the autopsy of which you performed on the deceased Jerry Bailey.

FOGEL: (Reading from paperwork) Okay. The subject was an adult white male, compatible with approximately 33 years of age. Measured 5-feet-10.5-inches, weighed approximately 180-pounds. Black hair. He was wearing a red and blue plaid pants and blue long sleeve shirt and a blue suede jacket. All of this which were blood stained. The long sleeve shirt had multiple tears compatible with a sharp instrument and the black jacket -- I'm sorry, the blue jacket also exhibited five tears compatible with a sharp object.

The clothing was removed. The body was examined. We then discovered there were 21 stab wounds involving the face, the neck, the chest and the back. Multiple blood stains of the hands, chest, and abdomen and in addition to that, he had lacerations of the upper and lower lip of the right ear. To best describe the stab wounds to you, I could best use a black and white drawing or whatever you would prefer for me to do.

Fogel then drew a diagram on the board, showing the injuries to Bailey.

FOGEL: The first stab wound I have marked -- these are in order of my documentation. In other words, when I use No. 1, 2, 8, so on, it has no reference to any interpretation of the sequence of events when administered. It's just for my own record. I refer to it as No. 1 and No. 7, and so on. Number one was located on the chest, fairly high above the region of the nipples. I call this No. 1, and this penetrated into the body into the chest going backward, downward and towards the center of the body which I call medial into the middle of the chest. That is what that one did.

TRUSTER: Doctor, might I interrupt you at that point and ask you whether or not in your opinion as a forensic pathologist, that particular wound and wound track could have been fatal?

FOGEL: The answer is yes, and why don't I just put an "F" on these I interpret as being potentially fatal wounds. That would have been fatal by the hemorrhage in the middle of the chest around the heart.

No. 2 was located -- if I may just draw the nipples for purposes of description. No. 2 was located immediately adjacent to the nipple. There was a superficial laceration. This was not a stab wound. I'm going to give you 22 numbers, but there is only 21 (stab wounds). This is not a stab wound, but initially I thought it may be, but upon further study it was just a superficial laceration. This is not a stab wound and would not have been fatal, of course. I put "NF" for non-fatal. I'll put "F" for fatal.

No. 3 was located below the left nipple, kind of to the side of the chest going up and down, and this only extended to the surface of the rib, so it did not penetrate deep into the chest cavity. By virtue of not going into the chest cavity, this would be a non-fatal wound.

No. 4 was located right at the lower portion of the chest and this went directly into the abdomen and, indeed, resulted in hemorrhage into the supporting fat of the intestines. This proceeded backward, upward, and medial. Again, medial being the center of the body, so, it went in that sort of a direction, backward and upward and medial. This would have been fatal -- a potential fatal wound. No. 5 -- I have to describe this on another diagram because it is the back of the body.

TRUSTER: Please do.

FOGEL: I'll write down the posterior aspect or back.

Okay, No. 5 is a stab wound involving the left neck, the posterior aspect of the left neck, and this was a non-fatal because it just extended into the muscle, so it was a rather superficial penetrating wound.

No. 6 was located on the lower neck getting close to the crease of the shoulder and this penetrated into the major vessels of the neck. So, this did result in significant hemorrhage in the region of the carotid artery and jugular vein and this was a potentially fatal wound that went down and deep.

No. 7 was located along the course of the shoulder and this penetrated downward, forward and medial, and entered into the cavity of the left lung, and by virtue of the fact that would cause the left lung to collapse, it is possible that could be interpreted as a potentially fatal wound.

No. 8 was on the tip of the shoulder and was superficial, was non-potentially fatal.

No. 9, I will return to this point in a minute, was a stab wound located on the side of the face -- and by the way these diagrams I'm using are my work records during autopsy. Of course, I use them for reference. I have prepared these by my own diagrams and dictation of a record that I have represented to both counsels.

TRUSTER: Both of us have been furnished a copy.

FOGEL: The No. 9 stab wound was below the surface of the ear and went directly back into the salivary gland -- like the mumps that would swell. That's where it went into, the salivary gland, nonfatal.

Going back to the posterior aspect, No. 10 is located on this portion of the back on the left side; I and this merely went down and struck the surface of the backbone. It didn't go any deeper than that. Since it only went to the backbone -- that was a nonfatal wound.

No. 11 was over here and went to the wing bone, to the scapula and again by virtue of the fact that it just penetrated on the bone, would have been nonfatal.

No. 12 was located lower on the back and this went directly into the lung, and because of that reason resulted in hemorrhage about the lung, and of course would have been potentially fatal.

No. 13 was on the opposite side of the back at about the same level and was quite superficial and penetrated to the backbone. For that reason again it was nonfatal because it didn't go deeper.

No. 14 was in the midline of the back, again did not go anywhere except hit the backbone and again would have been a nonfatal wound.

No. 15 was over more to the side, did indeed penetrate into the region of the lung, and therefore, could be interpreted as a fatal wound.

No. 16, getting close to the midline of the back of the body, penetrated directly into the liver, and for that reason would be interpreted as a potentially fatal wound. No. 17, 18, 19, 20 and 21were lower in the back, and 17 and 18 were going into the region of the kidney, but did not penetrate the kidney, so in all likelihood those would not have been fatal, 19, 20 and 21 were superficial striking the sacrum, the lower part of the back. For that reason all three of these would have been nonfatal wounds and the last one, twenty-two was in the very tip of the back, in the coccyx, and would have been nonfatal.

Fogel then went on to describe the number of wounds that would have been fatal and the type of weapon used.

TRUSTER: And, if I may ask you, sir, of the wounds that you've described for the members of the jury, and the diagrams that you've just indicated, then the total number of potentially fatal wounds would have been seven in number?

FOGEL: Yes, sir.

TRUSTER: Seven of the 21 stab wounds, one of which was not a stab wound, Okay, now, Doctor Fogel, you did then reach an opinion as to the cause of death at that time upon the conclusion of that examination?

FOGEL: Yes, sir.

TRUSTER: And, what opinion was that?

FOGEL: The cause of death was a result of shock due to the penetrating stab wounds, involving the neck and the carotid area, the lung and the liver.

TRUSTER: Now, at that point in time, please, sir, did you examine in any more detail insofar as an opinion to be rendered concerning the type of instrument?

FOGEL: I did, sir.

TRUSTER: And, do you have certain slides that were taken of the body of Jerry Bailey that would indicate in your opinion the type of instrument used?

FOGEL: Yes, sir.

TRUSTER: And, you brought those with you today?

FOGEL: I did.

TRUSTER: All right.

FOGEL: If I may just go back to the line drawing 19 for a moment and then make it a composite.

TRUSTER: Please do.

FOGEL: In order to establish what type of a weapon would have been used, it is necessary to look at the character of the wound, for example, a screwdriver would inflict a different type of a wound then a hunting knife or a penknife or household knife. Those are all different. With reasonable accuracy, we try to couple with that a probability of the type of weapon used. The way we go about that is by looking at some of the depths of the stab wounds to determine the approximate length, if a knife was used. If the knife blade was only two inches long, we saw a four inch depth wound, that would not be correct, so, based on the fact that the stab wound number seven, this one here which went quite deep, went a distance into the body of three and three quarter inches. Okay, stab wound No. 15 went a depth of three inches. No. 16, a depth of three and one-half inches. Now, using these as maximum sizes, then we would assume that the weapon would have to be in the vicinity of three to three and a half probably almost four inches in length of the cutting blade. In addition to that, we look at some of the deeper wounds and couple that with the length and it turns out that the length of the wound is this depth.

Now, let's look at the length as an example of No. 5 which was on the front and was three quarters of an inch. No. 10 was three quarters of an inch and 13 and 14 were three quarters of an inch. So, we'll project that the width of the blade would be about three quarters of an inch. The actual width of the incision was about one-eighth. So, what we are projecting is that there was a blade which was at least three and three quarters in length, three quarters of an inch in width and one-eighth of an inch in thickness. Now, the next point we raise is, is this a single cutting blade or a double cutting blade? If we applied that, (it) looked like a hunting blade, (and) then the character of the wound would be identical to that. There would be two sharp holes. So, this would be a double cutting blade. On the other hand, most common household knives have a cutting blade that looks something like that -- a single cutting blade. Now, when this goes into the body, what it does, it actually cuts it at three points. It cuts you here, here and here. So, what one sees is what I call an inverted Y. It is a Y because this is cutting and this is cutting right here. So, to demonstrate that you can see that here we have a sharp pull here and then of course a Y here and this of course is the reason why in my projection this is a single cutting blade. I have one more slide to show the same perhaps even shows it better. It shows the Y effect better. That's all of the slides.

TRUSTER: Then, Doctor, in your conclusions that you draw from the explanation you just gave the jurors, would you say that the blade involved in this stabbing of the body of Jerry Bailey would be one of a single cutting edge?

FOGEL: Yes, I would.

TRUSTER: And, would that be compatible with a household knife found in a kitchen?

FOGEL: Sure.

GASAWAY: Object to that. That calls for a conclusion not within the scope of his expertise.

JUDGE LAMM: He can answer that.

GASAWAY: Give us an exception.

FOGEL: The answer is that it's compatible with a knife out of a kitchen, yes.

TRUSTER: Doctor, did you notice anything else of any significance in your examination of the body of Jerry Bailey that led you to conclude anything differently than the cause of death being by multiple stab wounds?

FOGEL: I did not, sir.

TRUSTER: Doctor, do you have an opinion, please, sir, based upon your examination of the body of Jerry Bailey, about how long he would have lived from the infliction of these wounds until the occurrence of death from the time that they were inflicted until death which ensued?

FOGEL: Well, assuming that all of the fatal wounds were delivered rapidly, I would think that he would die within five minutes to ten minutes. He would die reasonably fast going into shock and quickly dying.

TRUSTER: Again as a result of loss of blood?

FOGEL: Yes.

TRUSTER: Dr. Fogel, insofar as the date of your autopsy, your observations that morning of January the 24th in the morgue, you did not do the autopsy on that Friday upon discovery of the body?

FOGEL: Did I? I did not, sir.

TRUSTER: Would you have an opinion, please, sir -- let me ask you whether or not in your opinion, based on your examination, your expertise that the time of death of Jerry Bailey would be compatible with sometime within Thursday morning, 48 hours prior thereto as -- as to the time of death.

GASAWAY: Object, leading and suggestive.

THE COURT: He can say if he has an opinion as to the time.

TRUSTER: Let me ask that.

GASAWAY: That's fine.

TRUSTER: Do you have an opinion?

FOGEL: The time of death is somewhere between the morning of Thursday and the early morning of Friday. That's a 24 hour span. I could not be more definite in view of the fact that I didn't do the autopsy until Saturday. I did not view the body on Friday.

TRUSTER: The body had been recovered Friday?

FOGEL: Yes, sir.

TRUSTER: Would you describe how you on other cases have determined the time of death?

FOGEL: The way that you try to determine the time of death is based on the stiffening of the body, the rigor mortis and the gravitation of blood to the dependent portions of the body. It turns purple, post-mortem lividity, the cooling of the body. There is an increase in the amount of potassium which is a metal found in the back of the eye -- a metal solution and by using all of these, why you attempt to come up with a time of death. This was in the winter time. Lots of other possibilities could interfere with it, and in this case I would not feel competent beyond saying that the time of death occurred somewhere between Thursday morning and Friday morning. That's all I can say. I cannot be more definite than that particularly in view of the fact I didn't see the body until Saturday morning.

TRUSTER: Thank you, very much, doctor.

After Heaver questioned Dr. Fogel, the prosecution rested.

The defense then presented their case, which was based on the fact Reagor was insane at the time of the murder. Their contention was that Reagor had to be insane, because the murder was uncharacteristic of their client and didn't make any sense.

Gasaway called Medi-vac helicopter pilot Steve McKim to the stand.

McKim testified to what he saw in the house and around the investigation.

Don Hayden, the Tulsa Tribune photographer, was then called to stand to testify to the authenticity of his work. He testified that the photos used in the trial were taken by him and published in the Tribune newspaper.

The defense then called Emma Gray to the stand to help validate Reagor's insanity defense.

Gray was sworn in and seemed to be apprehensive. Heaver picked up on that, asking her if he was nervous and assuring her everything would be okay.

Gray was an emergency room technician at Hillcrest Medical Center and, at the time, worked the 7 a.m. to 3 p.m. shift. As an emergency room technician, Gray's duties included taking vital signs, helping patients undress before examinations, transferring patients to X-ray, assisting doctors during suturing procedures and other tasks pertaining to the aid of the emergency room doctors.

She was towards the latter part of her shift on the afternoon of the murder when Reagor was brought to the emergency room by ambulance at around 12:30 p.m.

She said that she first saw Reagor after he was brought into one of the emergency room stalls and described the stall as "big as the jury box."

Gray was present when Lt. Randolph questioned Reagor in the stall and Heaver asked her to describe his ability to answer the questions presented to him by the investigator.

"He responded very slowly," she said. "A lot of times he didn't answer at all, like he didn't even hear the question, and if he did, you knew the answer wasn't appropriate for the question. His eyes were vacant and he didn't look like he could see anybody or respond to anyone verbally."

Heaver was finished asking questions and Truster began his cross examination.

After describing her duties in detail, Truster asked her about the time she spent with Reagor and what was happening at the time.

Gray said that she was helping Reagor get undressed when Randolph was asking him questions about the murder. Reagor's body was apparently limp and it took her around ten minutes to undress him due to his size and his inability to assist in undressing.

She also checked on him periodically throughout her shift and she that she probably had spent less than 15 minutes total with the defendant.

She also said that emergency room nurse Brenda Smith asked Reagor if he was hurt, but he didn't answer her. Also, the attending physician Dr. McLanahan asked Reagor if had drank from the can of floor cleaner found in the abandoned house, and again, Reagor didn't answer.

Then assistant district attorney Truster needed to clear up part of Gray's testimony.

"Now Ma'am, I'm concerned that, well, let me ask you this, is that the total response that you heard, or lack thereof, given by Reagor that day in the emergency room?" he said.

"I would say yes," Gray said.

"Then Ma'am, would you please explain to me, Mrs. Gray, how you can say to the members of the jury that a lot of the time, the answers were not appropriate to the questions, when there were only two questions asked and the response was to none to both? How can you make that statement to the jury?"

"I don't know," she said.

Under re-cross examination, Heaver asked Gray, "Do you feel like he was responding to questions from the doctors or the police?"

"I didn't feel like he was," Gray said.

Gray was excused and the defense called another Hillcrest Medical Center employee to help bolster their claim of insanity.

Eileen Hollands was a psychiatric nurse at Hillcrest and was stationed on 2 North in the psychiatric ward of the hospital and works the 11 a.m. to 7 p.m. shift.

Hollands did see Reagor on the day of the murder, but she first saw him two weeks previous on January 9, 1976 due to his overdose of prescription medication.

"He had apparently taken some medication in excess where it would be considered and overdose," she said.

She tended to him in room 2105 in Two North and described him as, "comatose or on the verge of comatose...No verbalizing at all, and he was really out of it."

After the murder, she also treated him on Saturday, January 23, 1976.

Reagor was restrained with leather straps on both hands, legs and across his stomach. He took in fluids through an I.V. and was catheterized because of the restraints. She also said that, "He didn't seem to have energy, he was very weak and he had trouble walking."

She said that his eyes were usually closed and when she lifted his eye lids to check them, they would be rolling around and rotating. Also, his urine output was low which could have indicated dehydration.

Hollands also said that Dr. Norfleet saw the defendant twice and there was no response, "except maybe some moaning."

Later that day he seemed to be in pain and was wrenching in the bed.

Hollands asked Reagor if he was in pain and, according to her, he was "grunting and moaning in an affirmative yes."

The strap across his stomach was too tight and needed to be loosened.

According to Hollands, Reagor's grunting and moaning in an affirmative yes was apparently the first time Reagor communicated with any hospital personnel.

Reagor communicated with Hollands on another occasion with a head nod. The night before his dismissal, Hollands asked him if he wanted a drink, and he nodded yes. She then bought him a soft drink. Hollands was excused, and the defense called Hillcrest registered nurse Sharon Dake.

Dake had been a registered nurse at Two North Hillcrest for about one and a half years and saw Reagor the day after he was admitted, which would have been Saturday, January 24, 1976.

However, it wasn't the first time the registered nurse first saw the defendant.

Dake was also working several weeks before the murder and attended to Reagor after his overdose of medication.

"He came in stuporous. At the time, there were traces of Elavil and components of Salonex found in his body," she said.

When asked by Heaver about his condition during his first hospitalization, she said that, "Well, he was unresponsive, then. You know, perhaps to the drug."

Heaver then began to probe further about his condition during the first trial.

Heaver asked "Would you describe Mr. Reagor's behavior during this first hospitalization please?"

"He was unresponsive," Dake said.

She also said that, "He seemed to be unaware of the surroundings and unaware of the people. He was unresponsive verbally, unresponsive physically."

However, she did admit that he did verbalize once.

"There was only one time when he said, 'Water.'"

Heaver asked, "Did he say, 'I want a glass of water?'"

"No, he did not," she said. "He said one word, 'Water.'"

Later during cross examination from Truster, Dake explained how asking for something by name can still be considered non-responsive.

TRUSTER: On this occasion, that is the admission from January, 24 when you first observed him this last time, did you indicate for Mr. Heaver that he spoke the word, "Water?"

DAKE: Yes, I did.

TRUSTER: And, did you get him water?

DAKE: Yes, I did.

TRUSTER: Did you feel, by that response, that you would characterize him as unresponsive verbally?

DAKE: I wouldn't say one word would determine him verbally responsive.

TRUSTER: Well, did you call him nonverbally responsive?

DAKE: No.

TRUSTER: Which is indicative to you that he was thirsty, true?

DAKE: Yes.

TRUSTER: Based upon that word being used by him?

DAKE: I would, yes, if he's spoken one word and that's all. I would still say he was unresponsive.

TRUSTER: You would say that, now. How about then? Would you say it then when you went to get the water?

DAKE: He was verbally nonresponsive. He did not respond to what I said to him. 'Water' came out on his own.

TRUSTER: Earlier you said you only go into these questions that you had characterized when a patient is not able to verbalize on their own.

DAKE: That's true. But, he --

TRUSTER: Excuse me, ma'am. Isn't that true? And, on this occasion, Mr. Reagor did verbalize on his own, didn't he? He said Water. True?

DAKE: He said, 'Water'

TRUSTER: Okay. You went and got it, didn't you?

DAKE: I certainly did.

TRUSTER: Did you observe him drink it?

DAKE: Yes, with my assistance.

TRUSTER: Did he pour it on his head or clothing?

DAKE: He didn't pour it at all. I held the cup.

TRUSTER: He drank it out of a straw?

DAKE: Out of the cup.

TRUSTER: Out of the cup? He didn't jerk his head away or anything of that fashion?

DAKE: I wouldn't call it jerking his head away.

Despite her testimony that Reagor only said one word the entire time she was in his presence, she also testified that he complained of being weak and dizzy. He would have had to verbalize those things in order for Dake to understand "weak and dizzy."

The defense then called psychiatric orderly Roger Clark.

Clark was a psychiatric orderly on Two North for three years prior to the murder and spent five years in the Air Force, including two years overseas running air-evac out of Vietnam.

According to Clark, his duties included checking vitals, temperatures, pulses and blood pressure.

He worked the 3 p.m. to 11:30 p.m. shift during the time of the murder, but didn't see Reagor until Sunday, January 25, 1976, two days after he arrived at the hospital.

On the stand, Clark described Reagor's demeanor in psychiatric ward as, "Completely out of it, there was no awareness and he didn't have much control of his bodily functions."

After the catheter and I.V. was removed, Clark said that, "(Reagor) urinated on himself a couple of times."

He also said that he saw Reagor around 18-24 times, and at no time did the defendant ever respond. He was also present when Dr. Norfleet attempted to communicate with Reagor, but again, there was no response.

The defense then called attorney Jim Goodwin to the stand.

Goodwin had been a lawyer in the Tulsa area for 12 years since receiving the ability to practice law.

The Tulsa attorney was contacted at his office on Friday, January 23, 1976 by emergency room doctor Dr.

Lawrence Reed at the request of Reagor's family, who had assembled at the hospital after the murder.

On the stand, Goodwin told defense attorney Gasaway that he arrived at the hospital on that Friday afternoon and went into the emergency room stall where Reagor was being attended to by hospital nurse with two sheriff's deputies on guard.

"He was very emotional at times," Goodwin said. "He would roll back and forth with his hands over his face, and he cried on one occasion."

The attorney said that the nurses were asking Reagor questions, but there were no responses. When he did respond, "his answers were nonresponsive."

Goodwin never attempted to question Reagor after he observed his non-communication with the hospital staff.

Gasaway then asked the attorney, "were you convinced he couldn't assist you?'

"Very definitely," Goodwin said.

Through a series of questions from Truster, it was established that Goodwin didn't have any prior relationship to Reagor or anyone in his family. He said that he talked with the Reagor family for about 15-20 minutes about possible representation.

The defense then called internist Dr. Craig Jones to the stand.

Dr. Jones had been an internist for 27 years and first saw Reagor on Saturday, January 24, 1976 by request of Dr. Norfleet.

Dr. Jones ran a series of tests to try and detect any possible abnormalities for Reagor violent behavior. He ran tests such as, red blood cell count, hemoglobin, white blood cell count, urine analysis, blood sugar, cholesterol, proteins in the body, chest x-ray and an echo-cardiogram.

Heaver asked what he found through these tests and Dr. Jones said that there was, "No organic cause for Reagor's behavior through these tests."

Dr. Jones also said that he saw the defendant for five consecutive days, and he was non-responsive the entire time.

He said, "I do not recall Mr. Reagor saying one word to me during my visits."

However, during Truster's cross examination, he was able to get Dr. Jones to admit that Reagor never exhibited any medical condition of "shock."

Dr. Ed Norfleet, a consultant at Hillcrest Medical Center, was supposedly the defense's big ally. Norfleet was under the impression that Reagor was insane at the time of the murders and was in constant need of psychiatric help.

HEAVER: Doctor, when did you first become acquainted with Paul Reagor?

NORFLEET: I first saw Paul Reagor on January 9, 1976 when I was asked to see him in consultation at Hillcrest Medical Center by his attending physician who at that time was Dr. Lawrence Reed.

HEAVER: Is Dr. Reed a Tulsa physician, Doctor?

NORFLEET: Dr. Reed is a Tulsa physician, yes.

HEAVER: And, what is his specialty, doctor?

NORFLEET: Dr. Reed is readily trained in surgery, but he does have a general practice here in Tulsa, but he's primarily been trained as a surgeon.

HEAVER: All right, sir, and, why did Dr. Reed ask you to see Mr. Reagor?

NORFLEET: Mr. Reagor was extremely depressed. He had taken an overdose of medication and had been in the hospital a few days prior to being seen by me, and Dr. Reed asked me to evaluate him prior to dismissing him from the hospital due to the fact that he had manifested some suicidal ideas at the time he came in the hospital.

HEAVER: All right sir, do you remember or can you tell us on what date you saw Mr. Reagor during that hospitalization?

NORFLEET: I saw Mr. Reagor on January the 9th, 10th, 11th, 12th and 13th. He was dismissed from the hospital on January the 14th, but I did not see him on the day that he was dismissed. I talked to Dr. Reed about him prior to his being dismissed.

HEAVER: Would you describe Mr. Reagor -- was the 9th the first day that you saw him?

NORFLEET: Yes, sir.

HEAVER: Could you describe Mr. Reagor's condition on the 9th day of January, 1976.

NORFLEET: When I initially saw Mr. Reagor, he was somewhat listless and apathetic and obviously depressed and had been admitted a few days prior to my seeing him due to the fact that he had taken an overdose of drugs and he continued to be depressed when I initially saw him and he was depressed during the time that I saw him in the hospital. He was improved to some degree when he was dismissed on January 14th, 1976.

HEAVER: All right, sir, for the record, doctor, which ward in Hillcrest was Mr. Reagor admitted to during that hospitalization?

NORFLEET: He was admitted to the medical floor, but I don't remember what room he was on. He was on one of the medical floors of Hillcrest.

HEAVER: Would you describe Mr. Reagor as responsive to you during that period of hospitalization?

NORFLEET: Well, yes. He was responsive, although he was slow, lethargic and apathetic. He answered and gave direct answers to direct questions, but during the time that I saw him, he was -- although improved at the time he went home, I think one could correctly say that there wasn't a great deal of spontaneity to his answers to questions. He pretty nearly answered the things specifically that you asked him about.

HEAVER: All right, doctor, did you see him at least once each of those days that you enumerated that he was in the hospital?

NORFLEET: Yes. I saw him at least once each day four or five different days.

HEAVER: All right, sir, doctor, did you reach a conclusion as to what diagnosis was rendered by you based on your evaluation of Mr. Reagor during your hospitalization?

NORFLEET: Well, he was admitted, of course, with the overdose of drugs.

HEAVER: Yes, sir.

NORFLEET: And, he's admitted, you know, with a diagnosis of suicidal ideas, and psychiatrically, we diagnosed him as suicidal -- not suicidal, a psychoneurotic depressive reaction.

HEAVER: Doctor, could you translate that and try to put that in lay terms for the jury and myself, please.

NORFLEET: Psychoneurotic depressive reaction is usually associated with a loss. A loss of some loved one, a loss of self-esteem, a loss of a job. Most of the time, it's associated with a loss of some sort, not necessarily something tangible, although it could be associated with the loss of money also. It's a time in which the patient becomes sorrowful. He becomes lethargic, apathetic and quite frequently feels like everybody is against him and doesn't much care if they are. They want to more or less withdraw and close the door behind them and withdraw from society during this time. A psychoneurotic depressive is the type of reaction we see with the young widow whose husband has been killed in Viet Nam or some war. They maintain contact with reality, but they become withdrawn and feel like they have nothing to live for, this sort of thing.

HEAVER: Doctor, did you find any symptoms of paranoia in Mr. Reagor during this hospitalization?

NORFLEET: Well, I found some symptoms of paranoia during this hospitalization which was more or less directed to the symptoms -- more or less directed to society in general, but there was definitely some evidence of paranoia.

HEAVER: Again, doctor, I ask that you define the term paranoia for us.

NORFLEET: Paranoia is where you have the idea that someone is against you, somebody is watching you, somebody has it out for you, and somebody has it to get even to you. You know, you feel like people are-- so many times people refer to it -- refer to paranoid persons as when we get a concern about paranoia when people start talking in specific talking to someone in specific single person which is more serious, but just the general paranoia is just talking to people — society, you know, who -- someone who is after you or you think - they think they are and they can't specifically say it, but they -- it's a person who really feels like somebody has it in for them and, in Paul's case it was more or less the system that had it in for him. He didn't feel like he got everything that he was entitled to.

Heaver then later talked about Norfleet's reasoning for getting Reagor back to work.

HEAVER: All right, sir, in consideration, sir, did you evaluate and meditate or discuss with the family regarding the benefits to be derived from Mr. Reagor leaving the hospital at that time?

NORFLEET: Some of the members of his family were there visiting from time to time when I saw Mr. Reagor, but I specifically -- oh, I might have talked to them in generalities or as they walked in. The only person I talked to him about discharging and future plans was his wife, and I felt like and she concurred in, that if we could get him back and get him to his job at teaching school, this would enable him to recover from his depressive state more than just letting him sit around at home or sit around in the

197

hospital and more or less vegetate. Oh, it was really kind of pushing Paul to get him back to work. She wanted to get him back to work, but before I talked to him, you know, this was sort of my plan, too. We wanted to push him along and get him back to work because we find that people get more enjoyment doing things that they had been doing or wanted to do and this enables them to recover from a deep depressive state more rapidly.

HEAVER: Doctor, are you saying by putting a man back into a job that he enjoys, the motivation concept helps relieve the pressure?

TRUSTER: To which we would object, leading.

THE COURT: Sustained.

HEAVER: Doctor, putting a person in an environment they enjoy helps to relieve their depression?

NORFLEET: Yes. We sometimes send people off on trips with their wives and their husbands and if they especially enjoy their jobs, they can come back to them and stop thinking about themselves and things that depress them.

HEAVER: All right. Did you make arrangements with Paul Reagor for some care subsequent to his discharge from Hillcrest at that time?

NORFLEET: Yes. At the time he was discharged, I told him after he got back to school and got things lined up in what he was going to do, I asked him to call my office and make an appointment. I sort of informed Dr. Reed when we made the discharge plans that Paul was to continue to be seen by me on an outpatient basis for continuing supportive co-therapy in regard to his depression.

HEAVER: All right, sir, do you know for a fact whether Mr. Reagor returned to the school in Sapulpa upon his discharge from Hillcrest?

NORFLEET: Well, I was not in Sapulpa and I didn't see him at the school. He did call me one day and informed me that he was at school when he called me, and I assumed he was that this was where he was, and as far as I know he returned to school. This is what he told me he was doing.

HEAVER: All right, sir, what was the purpose if you recall, of that telephone call?

NORFLEET: He called me in my office to make an appointment to come in and see me as we talked about prior to his being released from the hospital.

HEAVER: If you recall, doctor, when was that appointment set up for? What date, sir?

NORFLEET: Well, it was set up -- it was set up for the (day) that would have followed January 23, 1976, whatever date that would be.

HEAVER: That would have been January 26th, if Friday was the 23rd.

NORFLEET: That's correct.

HEAVER: All right, sir, when did you next have occasion to see Paul Reagor?

NORFLEET: I next saw him January 23rd, 1976.

Norfleet then answered questions about Reagor's demeanor the day he was taken to Hillcrest after the murder.

HEAVER: Was he, in fact, restrained when you arrived?

NORFLEET: When I arrived he was in restraints in bed.

HEAVER: All right, sir, did you examine the hospital chart from Two North, the entries that were made there at the time that you arrived about 6 p.m.?

NORFLEET: Well, no. I don't know when I first got there, but I talked to the nurse about what happened, subsequently, I examined the nursing records in the hospital.

HEAVER: All right, doctor, were they able to obtain a history from Mr. Reagor upon his admission to Two North?

NORFLEET: No, because he was verbally not responsive.

HEAVER: All right, sir, was he responsive to you when you first saw him that afternoon?

NORFLEET: No. No.

HEAVER: Did you attempt to question him, doctor?

NORFLEET: I attempted to question him for a long period of time, and he just did not respond verbally.

HEAVER: All right, sir, did you direct that he be put on any medication on the 23rd January, 1976?

NORFLEET: That night, but not that afternoon. When he was agitated I directed that he be placed on a tranquilizer but I don't know specifically which one.

HEAVER: All right, sir, would you describe, please, for the jury, Mr. Reagor's total condition when you first saw him January, 23rd, 1976. Mr. Reagor was slumped in his bed, pushed down in sort of a self-distorted position. He appeared to be dull with a dull look in his eyes. He was listless -- apathetic. From time to time he groaned unintelligibly. No meaning in the groans. He had attempted -- even while I was there, he did, to some degree, attempt to thrash around the bed as much as he could in leather restraints, and in thrashing around he had sort of pushed himself down to where he was in an uncomfortable position in the bed, and I pulled him up in the bed. He just kind of scooted down in the bed. This was the condition that I found him in.

HEAVER: Did you have occasion to consult with Dr. Craig Jones during Mr. Reagor hospitalization?

NORFLEET: I asked Dr. Craig Jones to see him Saturday afternoon which was the day after he was admitted to the hospital.

HEAVER: What was your concern that prompted you to consult Dr. Jones?

NORFLEET: Well, on Saturday morning I saw Mr. Reagor and I saw him with Dr. Lawrence Reed who came by and we suddenly noted from reading the nurses notes that he had not urinated since coming in the hospital that afternoon, and he had continued not to urinate and we kept having reports about sniffing something or having ingested some gym cleaner, and gym cleaner has some substance in it which can be toxic to the kidneys. We thought that he might have damage to his kidneys which was keeping him from putting out urine and I asked Dr. Craig Jones to see him, and in view of the fact that I thought he had kidney damage from which he might not be able to recover, and in view of his apathy and listlessness and not responding to any kind of treatment that we did.

HEAVER: In medical terms, is that what you refer to as a renal shutdown?

NORFLEET: Yes. That's what we refer to as a renal shutdown, renal, being kind of a highfalutin name for kidney.

HEAVER: Doctor, was Mr. Reagor dehydrated?

NORFLEET: Well, about the time that I called Dr. Jones in, I realized that he was dehydrated, that he hadn't eaten or drank anything for some undetermined length of time. I checked with the nurses and he hadn't eaten or drank anything since he had been in the hospital. So, prior to the time that Dr. Jones saw him, we started giving him intravenous fluids and about that time that Dr. Jones arrived, he had began to put out scant amounts of urine through a tube which we placed into his bladder.

HEAVER: Would you describe your next session with Mr. Reagor following your initial one on the 23rd of January, 1976? You mentioned you saw him on the morning of the 24th?

NORFLEET: Yes.

HEAVER: How did he respond to you on that visit?

NORFLEET: He remained almost the same way during the time that I saw him. Sometimes during that time the nurse would note that on one time or on one occasion that he had asked for water. This was the only verbal thing that he said or had done. He just said, 'Water.'

HEAVER: Did he not state a full sentence such as 'I would like a glass of water?'

NORFLEET: No.

HEAVER: All right, sir, did you see him again on the 25th of January, 1976?

NORFLEET: Yes. As a matter of fact I saw him several times during each of those days.

HEAVER: All right, sir, and, during any of those visits on those days, sir, was Mr. Reagor responsive to you?

NORFLEET: Oh, only on some occasions when I walked into the room, he responded in a manner that I felt like he recognized me.

HEAVER: At this point in time, had you made a diagnosis as to Mr. Reagor's condition?

NORFLEET: I formulated a diagnosis in that he was psychotic.

Gasaway then asked Dr. Norfleet about Reagor's malingering.

GASAWAY: Doctor, in your opinion, was Mr. Reagor ever faking any symptoms of psychosis?

NORFLEET: No.

GASAWAY: Any doubt in your mind as to that, doctor?

NORFLEET: No doubt in my mind.

GASAWAY: Doctor, I would like to ask you a hypothetical that's rather lengthy. I ask you to bear with me. Assuming doctor, that Mr. Reagor and Mr. Bailey left Sapulpa High School at some time in the morning between 8:15 and 8:45 a.m. in Mr. Reagor's automobile, in a manner which appeared to be friendly to third parties, and drove off, didn't come back to teach their scheduled classes that morning, and assume further, they drove around for a while, one hour or 24 hours, not really certain, but at some point during that interval of time, Mr. Reagor stops his car and they get out of the car, and assume that Mr. Reagor has a knife and he repeatedly stabs Jerry Bailey with 21 stab

wounds, seven of which are fatal, and then Mr. Reagor puts
Mr. Bailey in the trunk of Mr. Reagor's car -- his own car,
and he continues to drive around again from one to 24
hours, we're not certain, and he pulls up to an abandoned
house, breaks some glass, parks some 50 to 75 yards from
this abandoned house, locks his car -- not sure where the
keys are, goes into this abandoned house, no electric, no
lights, and we don't know what time he enters, doctor, lays
down on a burned mattress and just remains there prone
until he's found. Assume all of those facts, doctor, and
combine that, sir, with your observations of Mr. Reagor,
your knowledge of his history and your training, sir, and
I'll ask you if what happened in that hypothetical really
occurred, whether you have an opinion as to Mr. Reagor's
mental condition at the time that he would have stabbed
Jerry Bailey?

NORFLEET: Yes, I have an opinion.

GASAWAY: What is that opinion, doctor?

NORFLEET: I think that he was psychotic. I don't
know what time he became psychotic.

GASAWAY: Would he have been psychotic at the
point in time that he killed Jerry Bailey in that manner?

NORFLEET: I think. It's difficult to ascertain the exact
time of the psychosis. He was certainly psychotic closely
related to that time.

GASAWAY: All right, sir, doctor, assuming that Mr.
Reagor had stabbed Mr. Bailey on Thursday, the 22nd, due
to the nature of that very act, do you feel that he would
have been psychotic at the time that he killed Jerry Bailey?

NORFLEET: From my knowledge of Mr. Reagor's
condition, before, for him to do this, he would in my
opinion have to be psychotic.

GASAWAY: Would he have been psychotic when he
was found at the scene?

NORFLEET: From my observation of the history that I obtained, I would think he was psychotic when he was found.

Truster then cross examined Dr. Norfleet and asked him to write on a board the days surrounding the murder that Reagor was insane. Norfleet marked Thursday, January 23, 1976 and Friday, the following day. Truster then asked Dr. Norfleet to mark the exact time that Reagor became psychotic, but he couldn't.

Truster then asked Dr. Norfleet about his conversations with Reagor during his first hospital visit in early January.

NORFLEET: I asked him why he was depressed.

TRUSTER: Okay. What did he tell you? Why he was depressed?

NORFLEET: Well, he was depressed over the fact – one of the things he was depressed about, he had been an assistant coach of the football team at the high school in Sapulpa, and he had been depressed really during the season because Sapulpa hadn't had such a good football season that year. The football season had been so bad that there was sort of a demand to change the coaching staff, and Mr. Bailey who was the head football coach had resigned and Mr. Reagor had applied for the job and he thought that he had the qualifications for the job, but that he wasn't going to get the job, and he was depressed over the system that deprived him of getting a job that he wanted and of getting a job he was qualified to do, and he was depressed over his feeling that he really just couldn't or didn't get a proper shake, proper opportunity in that time of events in doing something that he really felt that he wanted to do and he was qualified to do. This was the thing he was most depressed about.

TRUSTER: Was that the thing that preoccupied his thoughts to your knowledge and formed the basis of your opinion that he was a depressed person at that time?

HEAVER: Object to the form of the question. It's compound, and he asked two different questions.

TRUSTER: I don't believe I did, Judge.

TRUSTER: Was that the guts that made him depressed, doctor?

NORFLEET: Other minor things, but in my opinion that was the guts of it. Those were the things that he was depressed about.

TRUSTER: Okay. He had applied, and by the way, did he mention it to you in that interview that another coach had already been appointed to fill the vacancy?

NORFLEET: I'm not sure that he knew that someone had. He knew at the time that he wasn't going to get it, but also to offset this, they had changed his title. They had changed it to where he had been an assistant principal and they called him a vice. He was sort of an, in my opinion, what we would call in a semantic promotion, not going to give you very much but-- well, I don't remember what it was. He was to have it was just to give him more he was have more oomph.

TRUSTER: Sort of like a dime used to get a cup of coffee type of thing?

NORFLEET: I think there was a little money that went with it, but the Sapulpa School system had, in my opinion, wanted to show him that they were maintaining good faith with him and they this was just something to frost the cake more, and Paul kind of looked at it that way too. It was kind of a promotion, but kind of a hollow promotion.

TRUSTER: So, in sum and substance, he was still deeply concerned about not being appointed head coach?

NORFLEET: Yes. He was concerned about not being head coach.

TRUSTER: All right, sir, now, you never did see Paul Jr. again in person until then the day of January the 23rd, 1976. Correct?

NORFLEET: That's correct.

TRUSTER: All right, sir, now, when you first saw him at Hillcrest, do you recall was that on Two North up there?

NORFLEET: I didn't really see him in the emergency room or talk to him in the emergency room. When I saw him he was on Two North or the ward up there on Two North at Hillcrest.

Truster then called Loraine Schmidt as a rebuttal witness to Norfleet.

Schmidt was a licensed M.D. with special training in psychiatry. She was a psychiatrist with a bachelor's degree and an M.D. from Northeastern in Chicago and had psychiatric training from Norman and Oklahoma City at Central State Hospital. She has been accepted by Oklahoma Courts of law as an expert in the field of psychiatry.

Her main function is to determine whether a person is competent or not to stand trial according to Oklahoma law.

Schmidt said that the first time she met Reagor was on January 30, 1976. During the 30 minute interview, Reagor did not respond to any of her questions. However, on February 2, 1976, Reagor responded to all of Schmidt's questions and "fully comprehended what I was asking him and answered me coherently."

According to Schmidt, all physical and mental test performed on Reagor were considered normal.

Truster then asked her about the conversations that she had with the defendant regarding Jerry Bailey and his mental state at the time.

She said that she first saw Reagor on January 30, 1976. The interview lasted about 15-20 minutes and Reagor didn't respond to any of her questions. She saw him again on February 3, 1976 and this interview was more successful.

"At that time he talked back with me and finally comprehended what I was asking him and he answered me coherently," Schmidt said.

The doctor said that while Reagor was at Central State Hospital she interviewed him for about 10-11 hours and she observed him for several more.

Truster then asked her, "...coupled with your observation concerning the testing that you did, the hours that you indicated for the members of the jury. Did you form an opinion as to whether or not the defendant had, at the time of the commission of the stabbing, lacked such mental capacity and reason to enable him to distinguish right from wrong as applied to act of stabbing Jerry Bailey?"

Schmidt said, in her opinion, Reagor was aware of what he was doing during the crime and while he was committed to several different hospitals.

Each attorney then got one last effort to dissuade the jury before deliberations.

During closing arguments, Truster's speech was all about accepting responsibility and that Reagor's defense of insanity and not understanding his Miranda warnings were just an "excuse."

He said, "Make no mistake, this was a brutal killing; 21-stab wounds, seven of which could have been fatal... Accountability, that's what this case is all about. Will you hold this man accountable and responsible for his actions?"

Truster said that Jerry Bailey waved at Steve Shibley while driving out of town. He had no idea of his pending peril. He didn't try to jump out of the car and run away. He had no idea as to what would later happen to him. Reagor wasn't insane. He knew what he did, where he did it and what he did it with, and he admitted to it.

He then asked the jury to find Reagor guilty.

Gasaway was up next with a last-ditch effort to get his client acquitted. He attempted to pound it into the jury's head that Reagor was not sane or in control at the time of the murder. He said, "It doesn't take a psychiatrist to tell that Reagor was insane...Reagor's behavior of stabbing

Bailey, putting his body in the trunk and driving all over Tulsa County was nuts… There was no motive. If Mr. Reagor had killed Jerry Bailey, he would have to have been insane."

Gasaway claimed Reagor felt persecuted and paranoid and, possibly, Jerry Bailey was the focal point of that, but the state didn't prove "who" killed Jerry Bailey.

At 2 p.m. on Friday, July 22, 1977, the case went to the jury.

The seven-woman, five-man jury were given the task of deciding whether Reagor was temporarily insane at the time of the murder, or whether he knew what he was doing at the time and willfully murdered Jerry Bailey.

In order to convict Reagor, the jury had to agree that on, or about, the 22nd day of January, 1976, in Tulsa County, he did then and there unlawfully, willfully, maliciously, intentionally and feloniously, without authority of law and with a premeditated design upon the part of said defendant to effect the death of a human being, to-wit: one Jerry Bailey, cut, slash and stab the body of the said Jerry Bailey with a certain sharp, pointed, dangerous and deadly weapon, to-wit a butcher knife with a sharp and pointed steel blade, which he, then and there held in his hands, and did then and there inflict in and upon the body of Jerry Bailey certain mortal wounds from which the mortal wounds Jerry Bailey did then and there languish and die, contrary to the form of the statutes in such cases made and provided, and against the peace and dignity of the state.

At 4:30 p.m. the jury notified Tulsa County Court Bailiff Bob Williams that they had reached a verdict. Judge Lamm and the attorneys were also notified.

As the jury walked back into the court room, making their way to their seats in the jury box, none of them looked at the prosecution or the defense. They just filed in one-by-one, and the wooden seats made a cracking noise as each one sat down. There was complete silence in the courtroom.

Over the past 18 months, Paul Reagor had managed to stay out of prison thanks to several hospital stays and legal maneuvers from his defense team, but time had now ran out, and time seemed to stand still as everyone waited for the verdict.

The defendant was asked to rise as the verdict was read. Reagor pushed himself away from the defense table and stood, keeping his hands at his side. He looked dazed and heavily sedated.

The piece of paper that had Reagor's fate written on it was handed to court bailiff Bob Williams from Judge Margaret Lamm, and Williams cleared his throat before reading the verdict.

"… The jury finds Paul Reagor Jr. 'guilty' of second degree murder…"

Reagor had stared straight ahead throughout the trial, occasionally batting his eyes. Several times, he had even fallen asleep during testimony. After the bailiff read the jury's decision, Reagor lowered his eyes briefly, looking down at the defense table before looking up again. His eyes made their way to the judge.

The packed courtroom showed no emotion and remained silent at first, but minutes later, a black woman fainted, which caused gasps and calls for help from spectators. She was eventually revived and treated by paramedics.

Paul Reagor Jr. was now guilty of second-degree murder in the stabbing death of Jerry Bailey. It took the jury only 90 minutes to do its civic duty. Apparently, they took only one vote, and it was unanimous.

The jury didn't need much time to deliberate, and there couldn't have been much discussion whether or not Reagor was guilty. They did not believe he was insane, and the quick verdict proved there wasn't much of a deliberation.

Judge Lamm then thanked the 12 jurors, and they were immediately ushered out of the courtroom after having spent seven nights sequestered at the request of the prosecution. They left quickly so they could gather up their suitcases, knitting materials, and books and magazines they had brought to the courthouse during the monotonous jury selection phase of the trial. Now, the 12 jurors, ranging in age from 19 to 78, could return to their homes in Tulsa, Sperry, Jenks, Broken Arrow and Bixby.

After the trial, Truster told the Tulsa World, "I am gratified for the Bailey family," he said. "Maybe now they can pick up the pieces and go ahead with their lives."

The defense tried two separate strategies, failing with both. First, they tried to get Reagor's three separate confessions thrown out because, according to them, Reagor never said that the understood his rights. Second, they claimed that he was temporarily insane at the time off the murder.

Apparently, the jury didn't believe either theory.

The convicted murderer was now looking at a long prison sentence. His sentencing hearing was then scheduled for Wednesday, August 27, 1977. Gasaway and Heaver immediately filed a sentencing extension, and it was granted by Judge Lamm and she rescheduled the hearing for August 19, 1977. Reagor remained free on the $35,000 bond.

On Friday, August 19, 1977, Reagor was sentenced to the mandatory 10-years to life sentence for the killing. His attorneys filed notice of intent to appeal, and Reagor then posted a $50,000 appellate bond and remained free while his attorneys worked on his appeal.

While out on bond, Reagor and his wife separated, and he moved back to Okmulgee to live with mother.

CHAPTER EIGHTEEN
Reagor's Attempted Suicide

Monday, January 22, 1979, started like any other day.

Paul Reagor Jr. woke up at his mother's house in Okmulgee. He ate breakfast and made his way to the front porch to watch the 18-wheelers drive by. Reagor's mother, Obzinder, lived in a house that sat only 10 yards away from the street, but that street was U.S. Highway 75, a highway that connected Oklahoma to Dallas, Texas. It's a north-south road that runs from Minnesota to Dallas and used as a major delivery system for semi-trucks to get products from one state to another.

There are several stoplights along the highway in Oklmugee, but they are generally green when traveling north and south because there isn't much traffic headed east or west. During the Red River Rivalry, the Oklahoma-Texas football game, most Oklahomans traveling to the game drive through Okmulgee.

That day, it was the three-year anniversary of Jerry Bailey's murder and around 16 months since Reagor was found "guilty" of the killing. Three years before, he had asked Bailey to take a ride with him in his car, and by the end of the day, Bailey had been stabbed to death and Reagor was passed out in an abandoned farmhouse. If he could do it all over again, would he? Is that what he thought about every day, sitting on his mother's porch, watching the trucks whiz by at high rates of speed.

Reagor stood up from his chair and started walking toward the highway. He never looked at the oncoming traffic and stepped off the curb and in front of a semi-truck traveling just under 40 miles an hour. The driver couldn't have stopped in time or swerved to miss the man with an apparent death wish. The trucker slammed on his brakes when he heard the thug of Reagor's body against the right fender of the truck, and the screeching tires could be heard several blocks away.

Paul Reagor Jr. had just tried to kill himself three years to the day that he killed his friend.

However, Reagor did not die.

Though seriously injured, he survived the suicide attempt but spent nearly a year in the hospital. Lengthy hospital stays weren't uncommon for Reagor since Bailey's murder, but he was always treated in psychiatric hospitals. This time, he was treated for physical his injuries.

After being released from the hospital, Reagor was sent back home to live with his mother, and he still had not served a day of his 10-years to life sentence, almost four years after his conviction.

Reagor's Death

The case was officially closed when Reagor died at his mother's home on Tuesday, July 2, 1980, 16 months after he was hit by the semi-truck and over four years after the murder of Jerry Bailey.

The day after Reagor's death, Truster said, "The case of Paul Reagor Jr. -- with all its confusion and bitter ironies -- is closed."

The Sapulpa Daily Herald Newspaper printed a story the following day that read, in part:

Reagor, 37, died Tuesday night at mother's home in Okmulgee of what his physician described only as "natural causes." His health reportedly had been deteriorating for several years.

Convicted in July 1977 for the stabbing death of former Sapulpa High School coach Jerry Bailey, the one-time SHS assistant principal was never behind prison walls... Reagor, who had served as an assistant under Bailey during the 1975 season (his first since coming here from Okmulgee), had sought to succeed him as head coach and Bailey had recommended his assistants to fill the vacancy.

After another successor had been selected, early on the morning of January 22, 1976, the two men were seen leaving in the same car from the Sapulpa High School parking lot. Bailey was not seen alive after that.

When the pair was located later the day in southeast Tulsa County, Bailey was in the trunk of Reagor's car, dead from numerous stab wounds. Reagor, barely coherent, his clothes splattered with blood, was found in a nearby farmhouse.

Police learned Reagor had been greatly depressed and was treated for an overdose of drugs 13 days before Bailey was killed.

Reagor had been absent from school on seven different occasions between Jan. 5th and the 16th, and it was later learned he was undergoing psychiatric treatment. He had left school ill at noon the day before the killing.

Tulsa attorney Don Gasaway, who represented Reagor, maintained his client was insane at the time of the murder. After several trips to state institutions, however, Reagor was ordered to stand trial.

After a Tulsa County District Court jury found Reagor guilty of second degree murder and ruling that he should spend 10-years-to-life in prison, the former teacher-coach remained free on $35,000 bond while his case was appealed... The second degree murder conviction was upheld in May in a disputed 2-1 decision by Oklahoma's Court of Criminal Appeals. A subsequent appeal was denied, clearing the way for Reagor's transfer to the state penitentiary.

The Tulsa District Attorney's office said Reagor's legal counsel was attempting to have his sentence reduced, and that, coupled with the summer vacation of a judge who was to hear the plea, stalled Reagor's trip behind prison walls.

Truster said today he spoke with Bailey's widow, Beverly, who still teaches at Sapulpa, and she told him, "I'm just glad it's over now."

In the news article, the medical examiner described Reagor's death only as "natural causes." His health reportedly was in decline after the guilty verdict and especially after he stepped in front of a semi-truck.

Soon after his death, a rumor had circulated around town, and it seemed to gain momentum the more it was retold. Reagor supposedly knew a doctor in Okmulgee and asked the physician to kill him in a way that would look like a natural death. It was obvious Reagor didn't want to go to jail. He had malingered, faking a mental illness ever since the murder and even attempted suicide so he wouldn't have to serve his time. It was just a rumor.

Reagor's obit (Okmulgee Daily Times)

Paul Reagor Jr. -- Funeral Services will be held Saturday at 11 a.m. at the Eastside Baptist Church located at 217 N. Osage, for Paul Reagor Jr., 37. Bro. Hollis Birmingham, pastor of the Church of Christ will officiate.

Interment will be in the Our Lady of Grace Cemetery under the direction of House of Winn Funeral Home.

Mr. Reagor died Tuesday evening at his home, 316 Wood Drive. Mr. Reagor was a retired school teacher. He was born March 30, 1943 in Okmulgee.

Survivors include a son, Paul Reagor III, and a daughter, April Reagor, both of Tulsa, his mother Obzinder Reagor, of the home, four brothers, Cecil Wallace, Los Angeles, Willie Robinson and John Reagor, of Tulsa, and James Robinson, Kansas City, Mo. Two sisters, Rose Turner, Tulsa and Delois Butler, Aurora, Ill.

CHAPTER NINTEEN
The Final Chapter

The judicial system that was successful in finding Reagor guilty of murder also failed in that he never served a day of his 10 years to life prison sentence. The trial wasn't a "who dun it?" but a "why he did it." Reagor admitted he did it – several times. The jury obviously didn't believe that Reagor was insane, which means they believed the prosecution's theory that he was malingering and the crime was born out of hate. He was also convicted in almost record time.

Due to his malingering, numerous trips to mental hospitals and the appellate bond, the convicted murderer was able to enjoy the freedom that everyone else enjoys -- everyone else that hasn't committed and been convicted of murder.

In December of 1976, almost a year after the murder, Ed Poston was in the Tulsa Christmas Parade on a float in downtown Tulsa. He looked out into the crowd and saw Reagor enjoying the parade with his family. Laughing, smiling and enjoying the festivities, Reagor never saw Poston, but the television newsman saw him. Poston helped find Reagor in the abandoned farmhouse, but this was a surprise sighting. In Sapulpa, the Bailey family was attempting to figure out how to cope with the death of Jerry, forced to spend Christmas without him. They were trying to navigate through the pain during the happiest time of the year.

Reagor then spent three more years out of prison on borrowed time. The fact that he was probably in his own mental prison is irrelevant. He was angry and killed a good friend due to a delusion. He got away with murder.

Most Sapulpans believe that people refused to talk about Bailey's death out of respect for his family, but several people close to Bailey have said that it was hardly that. It is rumored that Reagor was misled by the school's administration as to whether Bailey had recommended him for the job, and that misinformation pushed Reagor over the edge. It's been said that Reagor was flat-out lied to and was told that Bailey had not recommended him for the job. However, Bailey had, but Reagor didn't know that and let the hate build up until he decided to kill his former head coach.

The murder, obviously, devastated the Bailey family, but it also devastated three towns – Sapulpa, Nowata and Broken Bow. The teachers and coaches that got to know Jerry Bailey at Sapulpa were especially broken. The poker game between coaches held on Wednesdays at Antwine Pryor's house ended, and the coaches never really went back to the old watering holes they frequented with Bailey after Friday night football games. The Sapulpa coaches were lost.

They shared holidays and had family barbeques. Jerry, Paul and the rest of the coaching staff probably spent more time together than with their families. They spent long nights and early mornings watching film or drawing up plays. They spent hot summers and cold winters together.

Before the murders, Bailey was in his office looking at papers on his job-getting kit when Reagor barged in clearly upset. Reagor asked Bailey why he didn't recommend him for the job, and Bailey assured him that he did. Bailey had recommended all of his assistants. He might not have recommended them as individuals, but he did say they were all qualified applicants.

Apparently, that was not good enough for Reagor, who had it in his mind that Bailey was standing in the way of advancement. If Reagor got the job, he would have been the first black head football coach at Sapulpa.

If Reagor did confront Bailey then why did Reagor kill him? Was he again told that he wasn't recommended, or did he not believe Bailey? No one will ever know.

Beverly, Guy and Diedra stayed in Sapulpa and picked up the pieces of their lives. Guy and Diedra both graduated from Sapulpa and went off to college. Beverly remained a math teacher until her retirement in 1996. She died of a brain tumor in 1998. She was the cheerleading sponsor for years and an avid supporter of academics and athletics. Beverly could be seen at Chieftain basketball and football games, cheering for the players, which were also her students, and keeping a watchful eye on her cheerleaders.

Beverly had a run-in with Reagor a year or so after the murder. Beverly was enjoying a football game in Norman at the University of Oklahoma when she ran right into the man that killed her husband. Nothing was said, and the two just walked away. A year after Reagor murdered Jerry Bailey in cold blood, Reagor was out enjoying the same college football game as Bailey's widow. Several friends of the Bailey's have said that Beverly was terrified of Reagor after the murder because he was not in jail. She often asked Trooper Kent Thomsen to escort her and her family to events and functions outside of Sapulpa. She always offered to pay him for his services, and he always declined. Jerry Bailey was his friend.

Beverly re-married right before her death. She married long-time companion, Eli Walker, who was football star at Sapulpa in the 1950s. He graduated from Sapulpa in 1957 and was a member of the 1959 Northeastern Oklahoma A&M Junior College National Championship team. He also earned All-American honors while at NEO. Walker died in 2017.

Throughout the years at Sapulpa, football coaches changed. Some were good. Some were not so good. As time faded, people didn't talk about the murder very often, and then they stopped talking about it, all together.

Some coaches have streets named after them or are immortalized with a bronze statue. Some have had stadiums and fields named after them because of their ability to win football games. Jerry Bailey didn't just coach football; he helped a community accept people despite the color of their skin. He helped build a football program that had some of the worst facilities in the state, and he helped raise young men, teaching them about life as well as football.

Black students had stopped playing football when Bailey arrived at Sapulpa, and he immediately changed that. The new coach started talking to the black athletes in the school hallways, in the basketball gym, the wrestling room, and around town. They made every excuse in the world as to why they couldn't play, and he had an answer for every excuse. If it was a ride they needed, he picked them up and dropped them off. If it was shoes they needed, he made sure they had a pair. If it was clothes they needed, they never went without. He did the same for the white and Indian players as well. The only colors Bailey saw were Blue and Silver.

The Bailey Building is now, unfortunately, referred to as the Blue Building, and most students don't even know who the building was named after or why. It wasn't renamed the Blue Building. The football players had actually begun to call it the Blue Building before Bailey's death because of its color. Now, football players and students don't know anything about the coach or the tragedy that ended his life.

The Nowata High School football dressing room is called the Jerry Bailey Field House, and there is a sign on the building, leaving no doubt as to whom the building is named after. Nowata didn't name the weight room after him because he won the only state championship in the school's history. They did it because of the legacy he left behind and the lives he touched.

When Ronald James was the principal of the Sapulpa High School, he made sure that everyone called the building by its name out of respect for Jerry and Beverly. If anyone called it any other name, they were immediately corrected. When talking to him about the book, I made the mistake, and he corrected me. But throughout the years, principals, superintendents and the faculty have changed, and no one is correcting the students anymore.

For years, the only things memorializing the slain coach were stories from former players, and a small bronze plaque in front of the Bailey Building that read: "This building was built primarily by the personal efforts and imagination of one man. He loved this outdoor sports facility and chose to spend many hours here. In fond remembrance we the students, faculty and board of education of Sapulpa High School, dedicate this magnificent facility to Jerry R. Bailey."

The building was dedicated on Oct. 8, 1976 -- a little over nine months after his death. The shrine became a place where freshman football players sat, waiting for their parents to pick them up after school. The kids sat on the brick and bronze monument without a clue as to who Jerry Bailey was and why the building was named after him. It's not out of disrespect, but out of ignorance since no one has told them.

That changed a bit thanks to former Sapulpa Athletic Director Onis Panky, a 1974 Sapulpa graduate. Panky was an athlete and eventually a coach at Sapulpa and was named athletic director in 2008. When he got the job, several sports facilities were being remodeled, including the football stadium's turf and running track and the Bailey Building. Panky ordered big silver letters that read: "The Jerry Bailey Building" to be displayed on the front of the blue metal building that housed the football locker rooms, weight rooms and coaches offices. It took over 30 years, but Jerry Bailey's name was finally on the building he was so instrumental in creating. Hopefully, young players will start asking about who Bailey is, and hopefully, this book can answer their questions.

Jerry Bailey, in a sense, gave his life for Sapulpa football. It wasn't by choice, but he lived Sapulpa football while he was coach, and he gave everything he had for his players, his team and his community.

Bailey was named the Oklahoma Coaches Association Coach of the Year in 1970 at Nowata and was inducted into the OCA Hall of Fame for Distinguished Service, posthumously in 1985.

The class of 1976 dedicated a page to coach Bailey in their high school yearbook. Next to a large picture of Bailey, the class picked a poem by Longfellow and one by William Ernest Henley.

Lives of great men remind us
We can make our lives sublime,
And departing, leave behind us
Footprints on the sands of time.
                    Longfellow

It matters not how straight the gate,
How charges with the punishments scroll,
I am the master of my fate:
I am the captain of my soul.
                    William Ernest Hensley

The page also read: Jerry Bailey was loved and respected by those who knew him. A humanitarian: his boys always came first.

In his five years at Sapulpa High School, Coach Bailey accomplished innumerable things. He was responsible for the acquisition of the new outdoor sports facility due to his tireless efforts; work has also begun on the much-needed football stadium. With his easy-going nature and wry sense of humor, Coach Bailey developed a rapport between himself and his players. Under his guided hand a "togetherness" grew among the members of the football team.

Coach Bailey will always have a special place in the hearts of the students at Sapulpa High School. His influence on those whose lives he touched will remain forever. His mark on the community is one that will not be soon forgotten. As a Scottish poet once wrote: "To live in hearts we leave behind is not to die."

Four years after Bailey's death on Jan. 22, 1980, the Sapulpa Daily Herald published this article.

JANUARY 22: A DATE SAPULPANS REMEMBER

Four years after his death, the memory of former coach Jerry R. Bailey is kept alive in the Sapulpa community.

The shock of the popular teacher-coach's death numbed students and faculty at Sapulpa High School. Classes were dismissed. A wrestling tournament slated here moved.

But the shock is gone, and Bailey's contribution to sports in Sapulpa remains.

Each year, the Jerry Bailey Tribute Trophy is presented to the SHS athlete who best exemplifies the spirit of the popular coach – "to a student of outstanding character who is spiritually alive, intellectually alert and physically disciplined."

An athletic facility at the school, completed less than a year after his death, bears his name.

OKMULGEE -- It is January 22, a haunting day for Paul Reagor Jr.

Four years ago this morning the former Sapulpa High School assistant principal disappeared with coaching colleague Jerry Bailey, whose bloody body was found a day later near Bixby in the trunk of Reagor's car.

A Tulsa County jury convicted Reagor of second degree murder in Bailey's death and sentenced him to a term of 10 years-to-life nearly 2 and 1/2 years ago.

But today, Reagor, 36, remains free on a $35,000 bond, walking the streets of his home town, awaiting an appeals court ruling which may grant him a new trial in the case. He lives here with his mother -- his wife having divorced him, taking their children to live in another state.

He has never been to prison and spent only a short time in jail, although several times prior to the trial he was sent to state hospitals for psychiatric treatment.

"Most people who knew him before couldn't believe it when he was arrested," said one city resident who remembers Reagor during his coaching days at Okmulgee as being "quite calm, a peacemaker."

"Still there was considerable resentment when he came back here. It's just hard to believe that he's still not gone to prison."

Acquaintances of Reagor say he was employed by a roofing company following the trial and worked on job sites in several states. He has not worked, however, since he was involved in a truck-pedestrian accident a year ago, on the third anniversary of Bailey's death.

Police reports show that Reagor was struck by a semi-tractor trailer on a highway near his mother's home about 11:30 a.m. on Jan. 22, 1979 -- approximately three years to the hour after Bailey was stabbed numerous times and left to die in the trunk of Reagor's car.

"Witnesses said Reagor ran in front of the truck and lowered his head like he was tackling it," said Okmulgee Chief of Police Vernon Hodge. "He was injured, but apparently not seriously. He was back on the streets in just a few days."

Don Gasaway, the defense attorney for Reagor, contends that his client was insane at the time of Bailey's death.

"I think he was crazy then and I think he's still crazy," said Gasaway, who claimed he was unable to communicate with his client during preparations for the trial.

In his appeal of Reagor's 1977 conviction, Gasaway maintains that his client was not properly advised of his rights against self-incrimination by officers who found him in a vacant house near Bailey's body. Because of this, he says statements of confession which Reagor allegedly made to other officers should have been inadmissible in the trial.

The appeal further alleges that: the trial court erred in its admission of evidence concerning Reagor's psychiatric condition and in its instructions to the jury; inflammatory statements made by the DA in his closing argument created a state of passion and prejudice in the jury; the state failed to prove either Reagor's pre-meditation or insanity in the case.

Part of the appeal concerns a written statement by a staff physician at Eastern State Hospital which Gasaway says was "very incriminating" for his client. The statement claimed that Reagor admitted, in April 1977, that "he was putting on all his psychotic symptoms . . . His attorney had asked him to put on the psychotic act for three to four years and he was under the impression that the charges would be dropped."

Gasaway said the incriminating statement was admitted, but the complete hospital report was not.

The attorney also said his investigation "ruled out coaching jealousy" as a motive for the slaying, adding that he is still not positively convinced that Reagor murdered Bailey.

*****

The town of Sapulpa is quite different 40 years after Bailey's murder. The Bartlett Glass Plant closed, and the Liberty Glass plant has been sold too many times to count.

The town's population is about the same, and there are a lot of next generations that are staying in Sapulpa.

Bartlett Memorial Hospital was bought out by the larger Saint John's Hospital, and Walmart is one of the biggest retailers in town. The city annexed part of West Tulsa, and it's nothing but run down motels, truck stops, a sex shop, greasy spoon restaurants, and tons of crime.

However, there are a lot of big box stores in town, and several family-owned businesses are thriving. The downtown is still quaint with photography studios, clothing stores, abstract companies, and antique stores -- lots of antique stores.

The Creek County Courthouse is still in the same building, and it's always busy. The Sapulpa Daily Herald is now the Sapulpa Herald after dropping its delivery to only twice a week.

George F. Collins Stadium received a much-needed facelift with a new press box, home stands and concession stands thanks to a bond issue. The Sapulpa High School Soccer teams now have their own stadium west of town right next to the relatively new Jefferson Heights Elementary School. The Jerry Bailey Building is still blue, and his name now greets people that park in front of the building for football games.

Every year, people decided to stay in Sapulpa to raise their families, and generations are starting to pile up. It's not uncommon for former teammates to see their sons play together 20 or so years later. Sapulpans are hard-working, blue-collar, middle-class Oklahomans that do whatever it takes to succeed.

All of the Sapulpa teachers, principals and administrators from 1976 are either retired or have passed away. However, a lot of Bailey's former football players are still in town. Bailey stressed hard work and wanted the best out of every player he coached. Those attributes were around at Sapulpa way before Bailey arrived, but he demanded them, and they carried on long after he was gone.

Most people don't know Bailey won two boys tennis state championships while coaching at Sapulpa. Those tennis state titles are rarely discussed while talking about the few team state titles the Chieftains can claim in all sports.

Nowata has had its share of ups and downs over the past 40 years. The Ironmen football team has been to the state championship game in every decade since the state title in 1970, losing all of them. The town hasn't grown, but Nowata's residents are proud and they love their town. Their recently claim to fame is having the coldest temperature in state history at (-31), and a week later it was 79-degrees, which is an impressive 110-degrees higher.

However, they have a brand new state-of-the-art museum that tells the town's history from Indian Territory to now. The museum is located in the old Lander's grocery store across from the old train station.

******

On June 29, 1998, Beverly Bailey succumbed to a brain tumor after a difficult battle that lasted for about a year. Jerry Bailey was disinterred from Green Hill Cemetery a few days later and taken to the Broken Bow Cemetery to be with his wife. They were finally reunited after 22 years of being apart.

Oklahoma Highway Patrolman Kent Thomsen died Oct. 22, 2007. He worked for the OHP from 1969 to 2001, and was the man who first saw Bailey's dead body in the trunk of Reagor's car. He spent all night looking for his friend and found him the next day. Thomsen's son Todd Thomsen was a football star at Sapulpa and went on to punt and kick for the University of Oklahoma from 1985-1989. He was on the 1985 National Championship team.

Dr. Edward K. Norfleet died Sunday, Aug. 13, 1989. He was Reagor's doctor and treated him during several court-appointed stays as a consultant at Hillcrest Medical Center. He was under the impression that Reagor was insane at the time of the murders and was in constant need of psychiatric help. He would eventually become the medical director at Shadow Mountain Institute, a psychiatric facility in Tulsa, Oklahoma.

Judge Margaret Lamm (McCalister) died Tuesday, April 23, 1996, and was the trial judge during Reagor's criminal trial. She retired from the bench on Jan. 31, 1985.

Tulsa County Sheriff's Lt. Bob Randolph died Monday, Nov. 20, 2006 in Tulsa. He was in charge of Bailey's murder investigation and was the first to question Reagor after the murder. He read Reagor his rights and asked questions, resulting in a confession.

Donald Eugene Gasaway, Reagor's attorney, died March 21, 2012. Gasaway also loved officiating football, refereeing high school, college and arena league games. Gasaway argued that Reagor was insane at the time of the murder and the confession and tried to get it suppressed. He also made statements that the prosecution never proved Reagor committed the murder, and he even said he wasn't convinced Reagor murdered Bailey.

Diedra Bailey Knecht now lives in Broken Arrow, Oklahoma but still has strong ties to Sapulpa.

Guy Bailey lives in Hilsboro, Ohio. After working at Bartlett Collins Glass in Sapulpa for 15 years, he was transferred to Ohio to a wax plant that puts the wax in the glasses made in Sapulpa. Guy has several children, and his oldest son is named Jerry, after his grandfather – Jerry Bailey.

Coaching is in the Bailey blood. Guy didn't coach state championship football teams, but he coached just about every little league sport for his kids, and why not?

He had a great teacher.

OBITUARIES
Dr. Edward K. Norfleet

Dr. Edward K. Norfleet, 64, physician in Tulsa and Vinita, died Sunday, Aug. 13, 1989. Services were at the First Baptist Church, Vinita, under the direction of Luginbuel Funeral Home.

Norfleet is a native of Des Arc, Ark. He received a bachelor's degree from Baylor University and a medical degree from the University of Arkansas Medical School. In 1953, Norfleet began a psychiatric practice in Sapulpa and moved to Tulsa in 1966. He later became medical director of Shadow Mountain Institute.

Norfleet was instrumental in establishing St. John's Medical Center's Adolescent Care Unit, where he was medical director until retiring to Vinita in 1984.

He was associate professor emeritus of the University of Oklahoma Medical School in Tulsa and the University of Arkansas Medical School.

Norfleet was on the visiting staff of St. Francis Hospital.

Norfleet was twice vice president of the Oklahoma State Medical Association board of trustees, and a board member for about 17 years. He was a member of the American Medical Association.

Survivors include his wife, Almeta; a son, Ed Norfleet Jr., Amarillo, Texas; a daughter, Polly Norfleet, Tulsa; two step-sons, Steve Farless, Tulsa, and Brian Farless, Broken Arrow, and five grandchildren. Published in the Tulsa World, Aug. 15, 1989

Margaret Lamm McCalister

Margaret Lamm McCalister, Tulsa County's first woman trial judge, died Tuesday, April 23, 1996. She was 89. McCalister was born April 29, 1907, in Grand Junction, Colo. She was graduated from the University of Tulsa law school in 1944 and in 1947 became Tulsa's first woman assistant county attorney.

Newspaper clippings report that during her tenure at the county attorney's office, McCalister filed hundreds of cases against fathers who failed to provide for their children. She served in that position until 1951. In September of 1972 she became the state's first woman to be appointed a full district judge by a governor. In 1975 the judge made headlines again when she disqualified herself from hearing a lawsuit the Fraternal Order of Police had filed against Tulsa Mayor Robert J. LaFortune. She had signed the FOP's charter change petition and told the court she was "in sympathy with the plight of the officers."

She retired from the bench on Jan. 31, 1985.

Services were held at Moore's Eastlawn Funeral Home Chapel with burial at noon at City Cemetery in Tahlequah.

She is survived by her daughter, Mickey Stephens of El Paso, Texas; three grandchildren and one great-grandchild.

Beverly Bailey Walker

Services for Beverly Sue Bailey Walker were scheduled at First Baptist Church in Sapulpa.

Mrs. Walker died June 29, 1998 in Tulsa. She was born Oct 30, 1943, in Ardmore, to Troy and Estelle Standifer Edwards.

She graduated from Ardmore High School in 1961, attended Southeastern Oklahoma State University and graduated from East Central with degrees in mathematics and physics. She taught 25 years at Sapulpa High School and 16 years at Tulsa Junior College and retired in 1996.

She is survived by her husband, Eli, of the home; a son and daughter-in-law, Guy and Melanie Bailey, Hillsboro, Ohio; daughter and son-law, Diedra and Harvey Knecht, Broken Arrow; her parents, Troy and Estelle Edwards, Ardmore; and two grandchildren Jerry Ray and Guy Edward Bailey, Hillsboro.

Craddock Funeral Home was in charge of local arrangement. Smith Funeral Home in Sapulpa directed services.

Kent Thomsen

THOMSEN - Kent Douglas, born January 10, 1944 - deceased October 22, 2007.

Proud member of the Oklahoma Highway Patrol from 1969-2001. Devoted husband, father, grandfather, son, brother, friend and faithful fan of the OU Sooners.

He is preceded in death by: his grandson, Tal Thomsen; father, William Thomsen; father-in- law, John Fried. He is survived by: his wife, Jan Thomsen of Sapulpa, OK; son, Todd and wife, Melanie of Ada, OK and their children, Mene'e, Aneli, Tovan and Tyde, son, Jason and wife, Beth of Houston, TX; mother, Frances Thomsen of Norman, OK; brothers and sisters, Rosalie Mitton and husband, Walt of Lewistown, PA, William Thomsen of Houston, TX, Gayla Register and husband, Jim of Scottsdale, AZ, Cynthia Murphy and husband, Joe of Norman, Scott Thomsen of Norman, Tracy Thomsen and wife, Holly of Edmond, OK; mother-in-law, Ruby Fried of Oklahoma City, OK; brothers-in-law, Jack Fried and wife, Valerie of Del City, OK, Jim Fried and wife, Otie Ann of Oklahoma City; along with a host of nieces, nephews, aunts, uncles, friends and his beloved dog, Fritz.

Service were held 10 a.m., Thursday, October 25, 2007 at First Baptist Church of Sapulpa with interment in Norman. Smith Funeral Home.

Bob Randolph

Randolph was born Oct. 25, 1929 to Louie Robert and Sadie Adele (Farrer) Randolph in Hanson. He died Monday, Nov. 20, 2006 in Tulsa.

He was reared and educated at Hanson schools near Sallisaw. He was a veteran of the armed forces, having served his country honorably with the U.S. Air Force.

He married Bea Whistance on Aug. 30, 1952 in Tulsa. They had made their home in Owasso since February 1976.

Randolph spent most of his working life as deputy sheriff with the Tulsa County Sheriff's Office, retiring as a lieutenant. He had served on the Oklahoma Judicial Complaint Committee. He was involved in many civic and community groups, having served as city councilor and mayor of Owasso in 1994. He was a charter member of the Owasso SERTOMA, which began in June 1979, and was honored as Owasso's first Sertoman of the Year in 1984. He ran the Sertoma bingo for more than 15 years. He was a lifetime member of Sertoma International. Randolph was also a 32nd degree Mason and was dual member of the Tulsa and Owasso Masonic Lodge. He enjoyed spending time with his friends of the Liars Club at the Ram Café.

Randolph loved to spend time with his family, watching the grandkids play ball or participate in their activities, and especially taking them to feed the ducks.

Survivors include his wife of more than 54 years, Bea of the home; two sons, Bob Randolph Jr. and wife, Vicki, of Collinsville and Ron Randolph of Beggs; two daughters, Becky Martin and husband, Tom, and Rachelle Roberts and husband, Stan, all of Owasso; Sandy Juckett, whom he raised as his own daughter; 11 grandchildren; six great-grandchildren; five brothers, Kenneth Randolph and wife, Margaret, of Tulsa, Carl Randolph and wife, Betty, of Sallisaw, Jack Randolph and wife, Vickie, of Phoenix, Ariz., Thomas Randolph of Tulsa and Harvey Randolph of Texas; and one sister, Sally Dozier and husband, Charles, of Fulton, Miss.

He was preceded in death by his parents; and a great grandson, Seth Logan Randolph.

Serving as casket bearers were Robert F. Randolph III, Logan Randolph, Matheau Randolph, Ryan Roberts, Stan Roberts and Tom Martin. Serving as honorary casket bearers were Kenneth McEver, Robert Thorton, Bob Cullison, Buddy Warren, Frank Thurman and Art Lee.

Antwine Pryor

Alfred Antwine Pryor, 79, of Ardmore passed away on Friday, April 16, 2010 at Mercy Hospital in Ardmore, Ok. Antwine belongs to the Osage Tribe where he got the Indian name WA-TSI-KA-WA which means Dancing Horse.

Antwine was a graduate of Hominy High School in 1949. Antwine was an Educator for over 38 years. He was a member of First Presbyterian Church in Sapulpa for 48 years, and was a Deacon and Elder as well. Also, he worked in the church Soup Kitchen, belonged to the Locker Room Group and was in Northeastern Hall of Fame in 2006. Antwine attended 8 years of college at Northeastern University and earned a Master's Degree.

After completing college he taught various places such as Butler Missouri Junior High School from 1955-1956, Henryetta High School from 1956-1962 where he served as Teacher and Coach, Sapulpa Junior High School from 1962-1967 as a Teacher and Coach, Sapulpa High School from 1967-1970 as Dean of Students, Athletic Director and Counselor, Sapulpa High School from 1970-1978 as Athletic Director and Counselor, Sapulpa High School from 1979-1993 as Counselor. He was also Past President of Sapulpa Educational Foundation altogether teaching for 38 years.

Antwine was preceded in death by his parents Buster and Dallas (Christley) Pryor and a son, Mark Douglas Pryor. Antwine is survived by his wife, Dolores (Westover) Pryor of the home; son, Kyle Antwine Pryor and wife Alandra of Ardmore, Ok.; grandson, Justin Throneberry and wife Jamie; great-grandchildren, Shawn McClellan and Justice Throneberry; sisters, Mary Martha Frazier of Prattville, Ok., and Irene Jaeger of Shozlo, AZ.; also, many nieces and nephews. Visitation was Tuesday, April 20 at Smith Funeral Chapel from 6-8 p.m. Funeral services were held Wednesday, April 21, 2010 at First Presbyterian Church, Sapulpa, Ok. Officiating the service was the Reverend Craig Gibson. Bearers were John Wright, Jess Wright, Steve Frazier, Matt Haney, Iain Bell and John Cockrum.

Interment was at Green Hill Memorial Gardens, Sapulpa, Ok. In lieu of flowers contributions can be made to the church, Cancer or Heart Associations. Funeral arrangements are under the direction of Smith Funeral Home, Sapulpa, Ok.

Donald Eugene Gasaway

Donald Eugene Gasaway was born on January 1, 1937 in Springfield, Missouri and was welcomed into his heavenly home on March 21, 2012. Don is survived by his wife of 53 years, Georgann Simpson Gasaway and two children, Scott Eugene and his wife, Lisa and their two children, Katie and Ryan Gasaway and Patricia Lynn and her husband, Tony and her four children, John Thomas, Michael, Rachel and Carli. Don had two passions in his life other than his family - the Law and Officiating. He attended the University of Tulsa and received degrees in Journalism and Law. Throughout his 28 year career of practicing as a defense lawyer, he argued successfully before the United States Supreme Court three times and served as the President of the First Amendment Lawyers Association. Don's 50 year officiating career included refereeing high school, college, and professional football. He was one of a few chosen to work in the United States Football League and the World Football League. Highlights of his career were working the Blue Bonnet Bowl and the

Peach Bowl. During the later part of his life, he worked the Arena Leagues first championship game. A Memorial service was held on Saturday, April 21, 2012 in the Rose Chapel of Boston Avenue Methodist Church with a reception following the service in the parlor. Arrangements were entrusted to the care of Dillon & Smith Funeral Home of Sand Springs. This obituary was published in the Tulsa World on April 15, 2012.

Charles Dodson

Lifelong Sapulpa resident and former Superintendent of Schools, Dr. Charles Belton Dodson passed away on December 6, 2017. Charles was born February 25, 1933 in Kellyville, OK to Guy and Pearl Dodson.

A proud Sapulpa Chieftain, Charles was a standout in football, basketball and baseball. As quarterback, he led the 1951 football team to an undefeated season. A graduate of the Sapulpa High School Class of 1952, Charles later earned his bachelor's and master's degrees from Oklahoma State University. He began his teaching and coaching career in Broken Arrow and then Sapulpa. After spending a decade in California as a counselor and school administrator, he would return to his Oklahoma alma mater to earn a doctorate in education and then to his hometown to serve for the duration of his career.

Charles served in various roles as an educator, including teacher, coach, principal and superintendent. He retired in 1999, capping a 41-year career in public education. Remaining active in community and civic organizations throughout his life, he served as president of the Rotary Club, president of the Kiwanis Club and chairman of the United Way. Additionally, he served as president of the OASCD and president of the Creek County Retired Educators Association. He received a Lifetime Achievement Award from the Oklahoma Association of School Administrators and the Hero Award from the Area

233

United Way. In 2004 Charles was named Citizen of the Year by the Sapulpa Chamber of Commerce, and in 2006 he was inducted into the Oklahoma Educators Hall of Fame.

Charles is survived by his beloved wife of 60 years, Edith Sewell Dodson, children Becky Chandler of Bixby, Susan Dunn (Dale) of Sapulpa, Brian Dodson (Tracey) of Coppell, TX and Brad Dodson of Dallas, TX; sisters Jean Richardson (John) of Los Gatos, CA, Linda Eakes of Tulsa, as well as sister-in-law Carolyn Sewell of Flower Mound, TX and brother-in-law Gary Smith of Tulsa. He is also survived by grandchildren Julie Copeland (Chris), Heather Thompson (Garet), Jenny Gabale (Salil), Katherine Chandler (Kathleen), Lauren Chandler, Drew Dodson, Ben Dodson and great-granddaughter, Kenna Thompson, as well as several nieces and nephews.

Charles was preceded in death by his parents, Guy and Pearl Dodson, brothers Victor, Gerald and Thomas, and sisters, Dixie Dodson and Kay Smith, as well as his brother-in-law Thomas Sewell.

Funeral services were held at 1 p.m. on Monday, December 11, 2017 at Smith Funeral Chapel, 1208 S Main St, Sapulpa, OK. In lieu of flowers, donations may be made to the Sapulpa Public Schools Foundation in memory of Charles Dodson. The family would like to extend a special thanks to the staff of Storey Oaks and Rose Rock Hospice for their compassionate care of "Coach."

THANK YOU

I want to thank my family, first and foremost. I started writing this book, unbeknownst to me, in 2003. I was hired as the sports writer for the Sapulpa Daily Herald in 2001 and found out, almost immediately, that the paper did not keep any high school sports records. I then called Sapulpa Athletic Director Steve Shibley and asked for the high school's records. They did not keep any either. During the summer of 2002, I started scouring high school yearbooks and old newspapers for game scores and any bit of sports information I could find. I started at the Sapulpa Museum. They had a ton of Sapulpa yearbooks.

After pouring over those yearbooks, I went to the top floor of the museum to the old Herald microfilm machine. In the 1990s, the Herald donated their microfilm and the machine to the museum because they did not have room in the newspaper office located on Park Street. While I was looking through the microfilm, I reached the 1970s and saw Jerry Bailey's name. I was instantly reminded of his death.

My parents were raised in Nowata, Oklahoma, where Jerry Bailey won the high school's only state championship as head coach in 1970. As a child, I heard stories about the state championship season, and how my cousin, Dee Paige, was the starting quarterback. I also heard stories about Bailey's death. I was told so many different things. I was told he was killed, but I had no idea it was an assistant coach who committed the murder. I always thought it was an angry parent. I was told Jerry Bailey was killed by a screwdriver and his body was found in his trunk. I assumed it was his trunk, and I assumed the car never left the high school parking lot. The screwdriver rumor was told so many times that it became the main part of the story, and, during my research, some of the main players still thought a screw driver was the murder weapon, including some of law enforcement.

I just wanted to know more, and I wanted to be able to clear up some of the details for my parents. When I got to the Thursday, Jan. 22 edition, I saw the headline "2 Missing" and all of the blood rushed to my head. I could feel that my face was flush with excitement and my research started right then and there.

I started making copies of every article involving Bailey and I would read through each one carefully, attempting to answer all of the questions I once had, but it only led to more questions.

However, my work schedule was insane and I could only research the story sparingly. A year or so later, I had all of this information and decided to write a book. And here we are, 14 years later.

My parents have supported me in everything that I've ever done and this is no different. I couldn't possibly list all of the things they have done for me. Thank you, mom and dad.

Thank you to my aunt Cheryl Paige for being brutally honest. She was one of the first to read the first draft around 2004 and told me it read like a newspaper article, which makes sense because that's what I did all day. I went back to the drawing board completely re-wrote the book. Thank you.

I also have to mention my brothers Kenton and Kelly. Not because they did a single thing to help with the book, but because my mom will be upset if I didn't at least mention their names. After this book is published, I will be a published author and they will still be nothing other than utter disappointments to the family. Thank you, guys.

My children, Gabrielle and Paige, were the driving force behind the completion of this book in different capacities. My daughter loves grammar and she loves to rub the Oxford comma in my face. She helped edit the book and I am forever grateful. Also brutally honest like her aunt Cheryl, Gabby took a red pen to the manuscript, and I got the feeling, through her handwriting, that she was constantly disappointed in my very common and constant mistakes. Thank you, Gabby.

The book sat on a shelf, so to speak, for about 10 years, and Paige, my son, constantly hounded me to dust it off, complete it and publish it. He was also instrumental in the structure of the book and important changes that were made. He was usually correct in his suggestions. During the process, Paige also unearthed his passion for writing, and he is a really amazing writer. Thank you, Paige.

And, thank you to my wife Celeste for having absolutely nothing to do with the book other than the support and patience of letting me disappear into the research and the writing process. I love you more than life itself.

Thank you, Greg Stone, who drove me to the archives in Oklahoma City to copy court records, pictures, testimony and anything else we could get our hands on. He actually sneaked his scanner and laptop in so we didn't have to pay the absorbent amount of money the state charges for copies. After several hours of secret scanning, one of the archive workers gave me a box of the exact same records we were scanning because, for some reason, they had duplicate copies. At the time, Greg was the managing editor of the Herald, but left that job to focus on education and is now the provost of a Tulsa Community College campus. Thank you, Greg.

Thank you to anyone that allowed me to interview them for a story that is still obviously very painful over 40 years later, especially Jerry Bailey's children Guy and Diedra, Jerry Bailey's sisters, Terry Holbrook and the Sapulpa and Nowata coaches, teachers, students and football players that loved Coach Bailey so much.

Thank you to the Sapulpa Herald, Nowata Star and Tulsa World Newspapers.

I hope this book answers all of the questions the reader has about this case, the towns of Nowata and Sapulpa, and the short but amazing life of Jerry Bailey. However, the only question that may go unanswered is "why?"

Sapulpa Daily Herald
Thursday, Jan. 22, 1976
Friday, Jan. 23, 1976
Saturday, Jan. 24, 1976
Monday, Jan. 25, 1976

Tulsa Tribune
Thursday, Jan. 22, 1976
Friday, Jan. 23, 1976
Saturday, Jan. 24, 1976

Tulsa World
Thursday, Jan. 22, 1976
Friday, Jan. 23, 1976
Saturday, Jan. 24, 1976
Monday, Jan. 25, 1976

Nowata Star
Monday, Jan. 25, 1976

Made in the USA
Las Vegas, NV
29 March 2023

69825598R00142